THE PHYSIO PRACTICE
PROFIT SYSTEM

Five steps to more patients and higher profits

By Angus Pryor

CONTENTS

INTRODUCTION

1. Why you can't afford to leave your physio marketing to chance. 8
2. Making sense of so many marketing opportunities – starting with the big picture 12
3. What you really CAN do to market your practice (without falling foul of the government). 14
4. Three things you can do quickly to get the faster results . . 20
5. I need help NOW Where do I start? 23

STEP ONE: CHECK

6. Introduction to the *Check* phase 26
7. Average client value (ACV) – what's yours? 27
8. Time to sort the sheep from the goats – where are your new clients really coming from? 29
9. Who is your client "avatar" and why does it impact everything you do in your marketing? 31

STEP TWO: COUNT

10. Introduction to the *Count* phase 36
11. The fastest way to kill your physio marketing and how to avoid doing so 37
12. The one word that will slash appointment cancellations at your practice. 42
13. The simple way to handle your most tricky (yet potentially profitable) callers 49

STEP THREE: CREATE – STRATEGY

14. Introduction to the **Create** phase 56
15. The only three ways to grow your business. 57
16. Become a client magnet by defining your
    unique selling point (USP). 65

STEP FOUR: CREATE – INTERNAL MARKETING

17. Introduction to *Internal Marketing*. 72
18. Now that you know your ACV, how do you grow it? . . 73
19. Email marketing – the money is in the list 72
20. Client lounge marketing 79
21. Become a walking billboard for your practice
    without saying a word 81
22. Upselling – making it easier for clients to buy
    more from you 83
23. Total recall – terminating infrequent client visits 85
24. Lapsed clients – unlocking the gold in your practice . . 87
25. The number one way to boost client numbers at your
    practice. 89

STEP FIVE: CREATE – EXTERNAL MARKETING

26. Introduction to *External Marketing* 94
27. Building a website that turns browsers into buyers . . . 95
28. The large pool of "warmed up" potential clients just
    waiting for you. 101
29. Becoming best buddies with your local sports teams
    the fast and easy way. 105
30. How to get clients singing your praises
    (in a way that won't upset the authorities) 107
31. Using technology the right way to attract
    the right clients 109
32. Taming the ten-tonne titan
    – getting Google really working for you 111

33. Social media marketing – which options to choose
and how to maximise your return 121
34. Video killed the radio star (and other things) 125

CONCLUSION   **129**

INTRODUCTION

1. WHY YOU CAN'T AFFORD TO LEAVE YOUR PHYSIO MARKETING TO CHANCE

Physiotherapy in Australia has changed – forever.

Once upon a time, physiotherapy was a profession rewarding those who worked hard enough and were committed enough to carefully tread the narrow path to becoming a physio.

This meant working hard in high school to get an offer from a university that provided physiotherapy as an option. After that, there was a truckload of study in university to graduate.

Next came working as someone's underpaid offsider as you helped pad the pockets of the physio principals you worked for.

Once you had done your time in the trenches, it was a matter of taking out a lease, getting a loan from your friendly medical banking rep and then setting up your own shop.

While there were some challenges as part of this process (recruiting competent staff, finding a suitable location, getting your practice set up), basically it was a licence to print money.

Unless you were doing something pretty bad (according to AHPRA[1] there were only 12 physios de-registered in the past 12 years – one a year), it was pretty much a case of put out your welcome mat and wait for the customers to roll in.

Waiting times of three to four weeks for clients to see the local physio were not uncommon.

But then the party ended.

---

1   Australian Health Practitioner Regulation Agency

RECORD NUMBERS OF GRADUATES

Lead by political interests, the people got restless. While there were waiting lists of three to four weeks in urban areas, in rural areas, local communities struggled to source physios.

The first step was increasing the number of universities offering physiotherapy in Australia. At a national level, Australia was, in fact, producing sufficient physios. But they weren't distributed evenly, so there was a shortage in rural areas.

The answer to this problem was steady lobbying by local MPs and boards of regional universities to get physiotherapy added to their curriculum. And it worked.

With more and more physios on offer, pressures in rural areas were reduced as more physios moved to wherever they could find work.

OPENING THE MIGRATION GATES

A much faster lever for governments to pull (compared with adding physiotherapy to regional universities) was to open the migration gates.

For governments, this was the deal of the century. Some other country had already paid the high cost of training and educating physios – we just got to poach them.

And the best part was, these highly qualified physios had to pay to come into the country. For governments, this was definitely a win-win, particularly as many migrant physios make a significant contribution to the local community.

Nevertheless, these higher levels of migration have increased competition.

The opportunity exists for a range of corporates in Australia to get their fingers well and truly in the physio pie.

You see, as an investor (this is typically how corporates see themselves), physiotherapy can be a nice little earner. And the protection is good, as the barriers to entry are high – there is a substantial lead time to becoming a physio.

On top of this, corporates have been able to take advantage of a generational change. Australia is still producing plenty of physios, but for these younger generations, their career aspirations, on the whole, are quite different to previous generations.

For Generation Y, two years in a job is a long time. This is a group with a much stronger interest in life balance and as a consequence, a lower interest in owning practices.

This is good news if you're a corporate. Because, while Australia is producing plenty of physio graduates, those graduates are much less interested in becoming practice owners, which produces a steady supply of physio associates.

WHAT DOES IT ALL MEAN?

The upshot of these changes is pretty obvious – more and more physios. According to the latest data at the time of publishing, an extra 10,544 physios were registered in Australia in the past five years, which, by any measure, is a LOT extra. But what about the population growth?

From 2017 to 2022, the Australian population grew by **6.2%**, while the number of physios grew by **33.7%** – *more than FIVE TIMES the growth of the Australian population!*

A decade ago, there would have been no point even writing this book. It would have been like trying to sell ice to Eskimos – when there's no scarcity, there's no interest.

Nowadays, however, as a physio you simply MUST make marketing a key part of your business repertoire. It has become as important as the technical skills that allow you to practise.

2. MAKING SENSE OF SO MANY MARKETING OPPORTUNITIES – STARTING WITH THE BIG PICTURE

Of course, while it's all very well to identify the need to market your physio business, this process is easier said than done.

There are so many potential aspects of marketing and, confusingly, as many proponents of each.

There's internal marketing:
• this is marketing to your existing clients.

There's external marketing:
• this is marketing to potential clients.

There's traditional marketing:
• using newspapers, radio, flyers, signage and so on.

There's digital marketing:
• using Google, social media and a range of other digital opportunities.

But it never stops changing. What worked several years ago may longer work now. As tempting as it is to dive straight into what are known as marketing tactics, it's important to start with the big picture.

You can think of the marketing big picture as being something like the foundation of a building. Clearly, if the foundation is no good, the building will topple over.

When I was a kid, a song I learnt at Sunday School had lyrics that included, "The foolish man built his house upon the sand ..." and "The wise man built his house upon the rock ...". Getting your marketing strategy in place is like building your physio "house" on the rock.

At Physio Marketing Solutions, as we've worked with physios, we've kept a close eye on what's working best and what's fallen by the wayside.

The practices that have had the best results, over an extended period, have kept an eye on the following:
- insights
- integration
- innovation.

Many companies push individual marketing opportunities. However, we think this approach is incomplete and short-sighted. In our experience, it's only through a constant process of:
- gathering *insights*
- *integrating* marketing activities, and
- constantly *innovating*

that physios can achieve sustained results.

We worked for an extended period with a client who got this working so well, they had to stop advertising. They were booked out weeks in advance, even though there were plenty of other physios around.

With an integrated, innovative system drawing on market insights, the process for:
- generating more appointments
- achieving immediate sales and follow-up business

really can work.

In the rest of this book, I'll outline the steps you need to take to get your ducks in a row and new clients marching to your door.

3. WHAT YOU REALLY CAN DO TO MARKET YOUR PRACTICE (WITHOUT FALLING FOUL OF THE GOVERNMENT)

In this brave new world where physios are forced to embrace the vagaries of marketing, there is nevertheless an additional hurdle for physios to deal with.

For reasons of public confidence and protection, AHPRA has in place a number of rules about physios marketing themselves. Before we dive into what the rules are, let's have a look at why they're in place.

With a public health system that provides (some) Australians with free physio care, the government needs to keep a rein on costs. If you're the Australian Treasurer, you've already got a number of headaches around healthcare.

Well documented is the fact that Australia's population is ageing. This means the ratio of tax payers to non-tax payers is getting worse. If Australia were a physio practice, it's basically a case of billings declining and expenses increasing.

In this setting, you absolutely don't want health care professionals of any type encouraging people to use their services more than necessary.

If you and I were paying the bill for government funded physio (which, indirectly, we are), we wouldn't want a massive spike in the number of people getting discretionary medical procedures done, would we? So, who else wants a boob job?

TAKING THE FEAR OUT OF USING WHAT'S AVAILABLE

So, with all this restriction on your marketing, some physios have tended to take a very conservative approach. This is perhaps understandable, but nevertheless unnecessarily conservative (and uninformed) in my view.

Many physios steer clear of any kind of marketing, whereas, in fact, there is plenty of marketing that is perfectly acceptable without incurring the ire of the government.

> While I'm on my soapbox, you may notice I've generally used the term "client" in this book rather than "patient." This is deliberate.
>
> While there are some additional legal responsibilities of servicing a patient rather than a client, and sometimes it is appropriate to use the word "patient," I prefer to think of the people you serve as clients rather than patients.
>
> In my mind, the term "patient" infers:
>
> i. them needing to come to you, rather than you needing them, and
> ii. some kind of subservient relationship.
>
> In light of the physio environment that I've described above, **you cannot afford to think this way about your clients**. This change in terminology may be subtle but I believe it is absolutely necessary. Now back to the topic in question.

Despite what some physios think, there is absolutely no problem advertising specials for physiotherapy, e.g. new client offers; buy one service, get another service free etc. The only stipulation is if you're running a promotion, you just need to describe the terms and conditions.

Using these rules, a client of ours recently ran a Facebook promotion and generated 100 new leads in a month. All perfectly legal under state and federal laws.

What opportunities could you take advantage of?

REVIEWS ON EXTERNAL SITES

Similarly, some physios are fearful about encouraging client reviews. While there are rules around using testimonials on your own site, fortunately the policy does allow for some common sense.

Let's face it, if a client decides they want to leave a review for you on Google or on your Facebook page, there's actually nothing you can really do about it (except respond). So, it would make sense that AHPRA shouldn't penalise you for having these reviews in existence.

The policy states, "Practitioners are not responsible for removing (or trying to have removed) unsolicited testimonials *published on a website or in social media over which they do not have control.*"

With Google, I think you're pretty safe. It's obvious you don't control Google.

Technically, you can control the reviews on your Facebook page – you can switch off that functionality – but personally, I'd rather you leave it running until you're told not to. Any form of positive client review is a very helpful marketing tool.

So, how are the reviews looking for your practice?

WHERE TO TREAD CAREFULLY

There are a few areas you do need to be careful about.

If you're not a specialist (i.e. done an extra qualification and been formally recognised as a specialist), you can't say that you are a specialist, in your advertising. Rather than calling yourself a specialist, I see no problem with saying things that are factually correct like, "highly experienced with …, undertaken additional study on …" etc.

One area where you'll need to consider your risk appetite is around using existing clients to encourage friends/family/colleagues to become new clients. In this regard, the government doesn't like the use of testimonials nor reward schemes for encouraging referrals of new clients.

This is one area where I think the government has got it wrong. If we think back to the purpose of the policy, it's about getting Australians not to engage in *unnecessary* medical treatment.

I would argue, however, that for many Australians, physio care *is* absolutely necessary. It's almost always to the client's detriment where such treatment is omitted or delayed.

So, if you choose to play in this space, this is probably more about personal communication with existing clients rather than broadcast communication, i.e. keep any such schemes that ask for reviews off your website or Facebook page.

WHAT IF YOU DO THE WRONG THING?

So, what happens if you do go outside the policy? Firstly, let me say I'm not a lawyer and am not pretending what I'm about to say is legal advice. If you're worried, get some professional advice.

I mentioned above that from a review of the AHPRA website, only 12 physios had been deregistered in the past 12 years – one a year. None of the cases listed were deregistered, or even suspended/reprimanded, for advertising breaches. Not one.

In my discussions with AHPRA, they admitted that typically if someone is found in breach, they'll just write to the physio in question and ask them to stop what they're doing. This is consistent with my discussions with dozens of physios in the industry during the past few years.

I've never met anyone who's run the gauntlet and had any sanction beyond a letter telling them to behave (or words to that effect).

To find yourself before the board and/or in court is typically going to require repeated marketing offences against the regulations, particularly after you've been warned. In my experience, most physios are not even close to this situation.

So, if you're considering exercising your "risk muscle," you're probably best to partner with an organisation (like Physio Marketing Solutions) that regularly plays in this space.

4. THREE THINGS YOU CAN DO QUICKLY TO GET THE FASTER RESULTS

In subsequent sections, I'm going to dive deep into the full range of marketing activities that you have available to you. However, for the moment, here are three things you can do right now to get faster results.

FASTTRACK ONE

One of the simplest and fastest ways to get a result is to start measuring what's working now. For example, with some measurement, you might find that one of your marketing sources is way outperforming the others you're using. If so, look at how you can double-down on that method.

Similarly, the same checking might uncover the fact that you're getting little or no return from something that you're spending money on month after month. If so, pulling the plug might result in an immediate saving.

Having said that, there's growing evidence that it's the *aggregate* of marketing efforts across multiple channels that causes a client to first reach out to you. Therefore, on your new client form, ask them to "Tick all that apply" when asking how they heard about you.

After gathering data (and reviewing it) for a month or so, you'll start to get a clear picture of where your marketing is at. If there's no data coming in (no new clients), you've got much bigger issues.

FASTTRACK TWO

The second technique to use to get the fastest results is to set up a formalised client referral system. Referrals from existing clients provide more confident and trusting relationships with people who would otherwise be complete strangers to your practice.

If you can set up or formalise your client referral system, you've got every chance of improving your results in your quest for new clients. There are two basic models, which I'll cover later in the book, but in simple terms, you can use the carrot or the bouquet (no sticks needed!).

With the carrot, you can reward clients every time they refer, such as going into a draw to win something every few months. With the bouquet, you can send them something each time they refer.

Importantly, whatever system you choose, make sure it is (i) well understood by all staff and (ii) consistently applied.

Using the systems I've described here, our clients have generated dozens of additional clients in a very short time. The record so far is 100 additional clients in 90 days!

FASTTRACK THREE

The third technique is often overlooked but can be extremely effective. A great deal of data points to the fact that it's much more expensive to attract a new client than to keep an existing one – some studies suggest as much as eight times more expensive.

Yet, most practices, in my experience, don't market to their existing clients at all. For example, when you offer a new service, do you tell your existing clients about it? Do you communicate with them between appointments (other than to remind them of the upcoming appointment)?

For the quickest and largest bang for your buck, get these systems in place pronto and see how you can boost your returns.

As a case in point, a client of ours implemented a client lounge marketing system that literally has several clients a week walking into the practice asking for extra services. Slam dunk!

How much more business do you think you could generate in your practice if you were more effectively marketing to your existing clients?

5. I NEED HELP NOW. WHERE DO I START?

If you are in dire need of help right now for your physio practice, your first step is probably getting professional help. With a marketing agency experienced with physiotherapists, it should be able to cut to the chase and figure out the best plan of action to get you out of trouble quickly.

It's fair to say, however, that you probably didn't get yourself into this situation overnight, so getting yourself out of it quickly might not be possible. But at least you'll have a plan and will feel that you're heading in the right direction.

If you're reading this on the weekend and you absolutely *have to do something now*, then here is my plan of attack.

1. Figure out who your ideal client is.
    *   Refer to section 9 to determine your "avatar." The reason why this is so important is because it will focus your efforts.
    *   There are so many marketing possibilities out there, but you will waste time and money if you don't know *who* you're trying to attract, as different groups respond differently to different marketing efforts.
    *   Trying to be all things to all people is a recipe for disaster. The better you can figure out who you serve best, the sooner your books will be filled with *those* clients.

2. Get your Google house in order.
    *   The one thing that sets Google apart from most other forms of marketing is that clients have come looking for you. You didn't have to interrupt them while they're doing something else.
    *   Start with your Google Business Profile page (formerly called Google My Business). Have you claimed it yet?

Make sure there are lots of details about your practice there: services, opening hours, photos, even videos.
- Ask lots of clients for Google reviews. This is quickly replacing word of mouth as the best way for someone to tell what your practice is like. Get out of your comfort zone and ask.

3. Take a chill pill and get professional help on Monday morning :).
   - I don't mean to be flippant here, but if you want to get out of where you're at currently, doing it yourself by trial and error is definitely NOT the best way forward. You will waste time and money that you can't afford while you muddle your way through.
   - A good marketing agency, specialising in working with physiotherapists, will already have done the trial and error for you, and figured out what works and what doesn't.
   - Yes, you're going to have to invest a bit, but focus on how to get a *return on your investment*, rather than thinking of it as just being a cost.

STEP ONE: CHECK

6.   INTRODUCTION TO THE *CHECK* PHASE

Now that we're in the main body of building the outcomes of your marketing, we need to start with checking what's happening now. At Physio Marketing Solutions, every time we start working with a new client, this is the first thing we do.

As a marketer, such background research is invaluable. Checking what's happening now for your existing business provides the perfect form of market research.

I remember when I was at university studying marketing, it surprised me that market research didn't mean going straight to doing a survey or setting up a focus group. In fact, the data that your organisation already has is at least as valuable as doing those external measures.

Perhaps for the same reasons, our clients are sometimes surprised that we start by doing this internal research first. This is partly because most physio practices we deal with are hoping we'll just come in and implement a new whiz-bang gizmo that will generate outstanding results (more on that below).

Often, there's an expectation that to boost your marketing, it's a matter of throwing money at it. But the beauty of the checking phase is that it actually has no cost associated with it – apart from a bit of time and effort. Yet, done well, checking can be as effective as any of the dozens of marketing tactics available.

Why? Because otherwise it's like having your ladder up against the wrong wall. When you get to the top, you discover you're not where you wanted to be. That can waste a lot of time and therefore money.

As you embark on your checking phase, first cab off the rank is average client value.

7. AVERAGE CLIENT VALUE (ACV) – WHAT'S YOURS?

One of the most important metrics for your practice is a term called "average client value" (ACV). The reason this is so important is that if you know what your ACV is, you can confidently know what you can spend to attract/keep your clients.

I've done ACV calculations dozens of times with physios all over Australia and they typically fall in the range of $300-$500 per client per year. What this means is that, on average, each new client is going to spend that amount with you in the next 12 months. Some will spend more, some will spend less.

Knowing your ACV is very powerful. If you knew someone was going to spend $400 with you in the next 12 months, would you spend $20 to attract them? What about $30? You bet!

After all, ACV just captures what they'll spend in the first year. Most clients will be with you for several years – spending a similar amount each year. What a great system.

To calculate your ACV:
- Run a report for a 12-month period identifying spending by client.
- Sort the report from the person who spent the most to the person who spent the least.
- Work out the total number of clients on the report (e.g. 1000).
- Identify the median (middle) figure. For example, if you have 1000 clients who spent money with you in the past 12 months, from your list, take a note of how much client number 500 spent. *This figure is your ACV.*
- Write it down and revisit it every 12 months, at a minimum.

In truth, this ACV figure is actually 'median' rather than 'average' but for our purposes, the outcome is very similar. Later on, I'll show how you can boost your ACV.

8. TIME TO SORT THE SHEEP FROM THE GOATS – WHERE ARE YOUR NEW CLIENTS REALLY COMING FROM?

Another important part of the *Check* phase is to determine where your new clients are coming from. Most physios I deal with have a bit of an idea but don't always really know.

One distinction I would make here is about determining not just where your *clients* are coming from, but also where your *enquiries* are coming from.

Unless you convert 100% of your enquiries into clients (in which case, please get in touch with me immediately – you must be doing something very right!), enquiry data and new client data is NOT the same.

Most physios don't measure the source of enquiries at the time of the call – this is a mistake.

Part of the reason why this data is so important is it can shine the light on some really glaring issues. For example:
- I had a client whose practice was on the main street in a capital city where thousands of cars drove by every day. After three months of measuring their client source data, not one single new patient mentioned drive by or signage as what prompted them to get in touch – not one.

Message: your signage is NOT working.
- I had another client for whom this client source data showed, in relation to a magazine they were advertising with every month, that it hadn't generated a single new patient.

Message: stop advertising in the magazine.
- For one client, client source data showed that a whopping 30% of their new patients were being sourced by signage/walk-by.

Message: you're doing something very right; maybe you can boost it even more?

The final piece of the puzzle here is to compare your data with industry norms. At Physio Marketing Solutions, we have our clients capturing data by asking enquiries how they heard about the business, then we add the data together.

Each month, our clients can receive their own data back PLUS industry data. This can be an excellent eye-opener in terms of how your practice is going, compared to others.

9. WHO IS YOUR CLIENT "AVATAR" AND WHY DOES IT IMPACT EVERYTHING YOU DO IN YOUR MARKETING?

For many of us, when we think of "avatar" we have visions of a tall, blue creature with pointy ears (courtesy of James Cameron). However, in marketing, an avatar is quite a different thing but no less compelling.

In simple terms, your avatar is the ideal client for your practice. For some of you reading this, you may be tempted to think that your ideal client is anyone who pays you money for doing what you do!

While that can be true in the early stages of your business, as your practice matures, you should focus in on your avatar.

During the many times I've presented this concept at live events, I can almost hear the gasps from some members of the audience.

To the novice business owner, the idea of somehow favouring one group of clients over another immediately infers that you're going to *miss out*, by not servicing the other group as effectively. **The reverse is actually true.**

To take an example from outside the physio industry, think about a company like BMW. As a big multi-national, they have spent an absolute fortune in market research working out who is the ideal client for their product.

All of their marketing is designed with this avatar in mind. As you might imagine for BMW, they're focusing on a person who:
- is in the age range of 30-50 (Mercedes on the other hand, tends to have an older demographic)
- has a mid to upper income

- has at least an undergraduate degree
- cares about their image.

The more effectively BMW can appeal to this demographic in their marketing, the better their sales will be – BMW sold 2.4 million cars in 2022!

Now here's an important point: do you think just because someone sits outside the avatar, they won't still buy a BMW? The reality is people outside the avatar still buy.

Even in suburbs with a lower socio-economic population, some people still buy BMWs.

As another example, one of my favourite podcasts that I listen to regularly is designed specifically for women! Another one is for 20-year-old males, and I've spent thousands of dollars on their educational products. Rest assured, I am neither a woman nor a 20-year-old male!

Trying to be all things to all people is a *recipe for failure*. Instead, focus clearly on your avatar, and you'll sell *more* to people in that group (these are clients you want), but still get sales from outside that group.

This bears repeating from a different angle:

> If you're not focusing on better servicing your practice avatar, you're losing business!

A physio client of ours realised that he was trying to be all things to all people. Once he stopped doing that and focused on servicing a particular part of the market really, really well, his business grew exponentially.

This growth was from an annual turnover of a few hundred thousand dollars a year to multi-millions a year. Yes, avatar matters!

I have one final point on avatars before we work out how to calculate them. Whether you want to focus on your avatar or not, the fact is *your practice has an avatar already*.

By virtue of who's already spending money with you, your current avatar is already in effect. Why not just ride in the direction of the existing wave rather than struggling in the opposite direction!

HOW TO CALCULATE YOUR AVATAR

Run the same report that you used to calculate your ACV. (You did do it, didn't you? If not, go back and do it – you'll be glad you did.) But to recap:
- Run a report over 12 months identifying spending by client.
- Sort the report from the person who spent the most to the person who spent the least.

And this is where we do something different:
- Have a look through your top 20-30 clients and cross off clients that fail the likeability test.
- Just because someone spends plenty with you doesn't mean they need to fall into your avatar – life's too short to consistently deal with people you don't enjoy servicing.
- With the remaining list, identify the common characteristics of those clients having regard to:
  - o age
  - o gender
  - o family composition
  - o locality
  - o ethnic background
  - o occupation type/income level
  - o education level
  - o hobbies/interests

There will be a spectrum of answers for each category but, nevertheless, some common themes. Your job is to identify these data concentrations and create the avatar persona on that basis.

Once you've identified your avatar, there are two remaining steps. Firstly, I think it's a good idea to give this person a name. e.g. Sally, Mick or Rajeev etc.

Next, it would be really helpful to actually get a picture of this person. If you're artistic, you can come up with something yourself but otherwise, head to www.avatarmaker.com and create a free (animated) picture of your avatar.

Next, print out the picture, put it up in your tea room, office etc and think about that person in regard to your marketing activities, i.e.:
- "How would Sally react to this promotion?"
- "What would Sally think about the services we offer?"
- "How would Sally feel about the vibe we've created, the look and feel of the practice, our opening hours etc?"

Bottom line: avatar is really important and getting it in place can have a huge effect on your marketing activities, both in terms of what you do and how effective they are. If it all seems too hard, you may need to get some professional help to take advantage of this opportunity.

STEP TWO: COUNT

10. INTRODUCTION TO THE *COUNT* PHASE

Now that you've done your checking of what's been happening in your practice, it's time to get counting. This is where you're monitoring what's happening going forward.

The number one complaint I get from most physios about marketing is they don't really know what's working and what's not. It's really only by systematic counting that you can get a strong sense of the return on your investment.

There is some discipline involved in counting but the rewards are worth the effort. Otherwise, it would be like driving on a highway without a speedometer:

- You hope you're driving fast enough so you arrive at your destination quickly, but
- you don't drive so fast that you risk the wheels falling off (or getting a speeding ticket).

In this part, you're going to remove that doubt by counting. And one of the main areas to be counted relates to the precise location where business comes into your practice.

11. THE FASTEST WAY TO KILL YOUR PHYSIO MARKETING AND HOW TO AVOID DOING SO

A physio practice has so many moving parts that it can be hard for a busy physio to keep track of them all. However, if you're not keeping a close eye on how your phone is being answered, you may be inadvertently killing the results of your marketing.

It can be hard to remember what it's like for someone who is considering becoming a client, but remember you must.

In fact, periodically, get a friend or family member to go through the new client process then quiz them on their experience. I'll bet you a bottle of champers, they'll identify something you hadn't thought of that could make the process better/easier for them.

MARKETING SCENT

There is a concept known as "marketing scent" which needs to be consistent throughout the entire process for prospective clients. As they interact with each part of your business, (e.g. website, phone, face-to-face etc) each part needs a similar "scent."

Your website should portray your practice in a positive way that connects with the prospective client. However, if the aura from the website is professional and friendly, but your phone is answered only with "Hello?" (with attitude), you've immediately lost that scent for the client.

Similarly, if your website and phone manner are great but your premises are dirty, messy or in dire need of renovations, that scent can disappear within seconds.

This scent disconnect can kill the results of your marketing, and the client is less likely to make an appointment (or remain a client). Of all the possible disconnects, in my experience, it's phone technique that is fastest way to kill the results of your marketing.

PHONE TECHNIQUE

I was sitting in a physio practice recently when I overheard one of the staff members calling clients who had appointments the following day. This was a good start. Calling clients to remind them about their appointments is more effective than sending a text message or email.

Anyway, the receptionist (we'll call her Jessica) used basically the same script for each of the six calls I heard her make. Her script started well: "Hi, it's Jessica from XYZ Physio. Can I speak to Mr Jones please?"

She then stated: "I'm calling to confirm your appointment for tomorrow." So far so good. But then she said something that I reeled at: "Are you going to come?" Yikes!

The problem here was the in-built assumption that the client may not come. Worse than that was when one client had indicated they weren't going to come, Jessica asked if the client would like to make another appointment. The client indicated no, and the call finished shortly thereafter.

This was a clear case of giving clients a reason not to attend and undoing the efforts of previous marketing. Marketing 1, call handling 0.

KILLING YOUR MARKETING IN TWO MINUTES

I recently rang around 10 physio practices for a client of mine. We were inviting the practices to a free CPD[2] event (nothing salesy) and I completed the 10 calls in about 20 minutes.

What really shocked me was the lingering impression I had from each practice. After calling 10 practices in quick succession, they quickly fell into one of three buckets:

- practices that I would be happy to be a client of – I felt welcomed and listened to by a friendly staff member
- practices that were so-so – I'd go if I got a recommendation, or if they were very close by I might consider making a first visit, but otherwise, I wasn't about to become a client
- practices I would NEVER go to as a client.

Don't you think that's unbelievable? After just one or two minutes on the phone with several practices, I had formed the clear impression I never wanted to do business with them.

What is the message being delivered (perhaps inadvertently) by how the phone is answered at *your* practice?

HOW TO STOP THE SLAUGHTER

To avoid killing the marketing at your practice, you need to put in place a system for measuring call conversions. This means counting the number of calls received each day from new clients and counting the portion of them that make appointments.

This will give you an idea pretty quickly of whether your phone technique is helping or hindering your other marketing efforts.

---

2   Continuing Professional Development

At Physio Marketing Solutions, we do this as a matter of course. The worst I've seen is a 50% call conversion rate. The best I've seen is 90%.

Those numbers may sound alarming enough, but that's only the tip of the iceberg when you look at the implications of this over a longer period. In the previous section, we identified that ACV for Australian physios is in the range of $300-$500 per annum. For the purpose of this calculation, let's use $400 as ACV.

If your practice gets 10 calls a week from prospective new clients, that means effectively a potential $4000 in combined ACV (10 clients x $400/client) if they converted at 100%. Multiply this by 50 weeks of the year (you're allowed some time off), and this is $200,000 in combined ACV arriving each year ...

but only if you're converting at 100%.

For a practice that is converting at 50%, they are effectively leaving $100,000 on the table each year. $100,000! If they increase their call conversion by just 20% – from 50% to 70% – this means an extra $40,000 each year.

Yep, these numbers are definitely worth looking at.

WHAT ELSE CAN YOU DO?

Curiously, the mere fact of measuring your call conversions will make them increase. There is a universal principal that says: "What's measured is done."

Once you start measuring call conversions, this may also shine the light on other issues that need addressing such as:
- properly resourcing your phone answering to (i) avoid missed calls and (ii) get a higher call conversion rate

- making sure that the person answering the phone is NOT the least trained person in the office. i.e. "What do we do with Jenny while she learns her job?" "Well, at least can she answer the phone?" In light of the above data, I can only say "Nooooooooooo!"

To ensure that practices are not killing their marketing, at Physio Marketing Solutions we have developed the "CallTrackerHQ" system. Most clients using this system achieve a 20-30% increase in call conversions.

I wonder how much business your practice might be missing out on via your phones?

12. THE ONE WORD THAT WILL SLASH APPOINTMENT CANCELLATIONS AT YOUR PRACTICE

As part of this *Count* phase, one area that can really undermine the effectiveness of your marketing is cancellations.

Let's call them what they are. Cancellations from clients can be a giant pain in the butt.

With a service-based business, there is just no way of getting back the time that's been lost. It's like an aeroplane that takes off with empty seats. For physios, cancellations mean empty appointments, lost revenue and lower productivity.

IT'S ALL ABOUT IMPORTANCE

The fundamental issue that causes most cancelled appointments is the relative **lack of importance** that cancelling clients place on their physio appointment. Ninety nine percent of the time, if they really wanted/needed an appointment, they would attend.

Consider this scenario:

> Let's imagine you won a competition that gave you 45 minutes with your most favourite person in the whole world, dead or alive. It could be a favourite actor/sports star/business guru/ family member etc.
>
> Do you think you wouldn't do **everything you possibly could**, regardless of sickness, work commitments etc to make that appointment? Of course, you would.

The reason why is because you would see that opportunity as unlikely ever to be repeated and as highly valuable.

Therefore, building up a sense of importance for a physio appointment is really, really important!

The other message here is that it's the work you do *at the time of booking the appointment* that impacts how likely someone is to keep the appointment.

SO, WHAT'S THE WORD?

If there was a word that could slash cancellations at your practice it would be **scarcity**. Simple but true.

You see, there's more to scarcity than meets the eye. One of the ways we undermine importance is what we tell clients about the appointment.

If a client calls up for an appointment and you leave it entirely up to *them* what time they want to come, you've already inferred that there are lots of appointments available.

A lack of scarcity creates a lack of importance.

The less important a client believes the appointment is, the less likely they are to keep it. So, instead of asking the client what appointment time/day they want, give them a maximum of two options:
- "James is very busy, but we can either fit you in at 10am on Tuesday or 3pm on Thursday. Which would you prefer?"

And don't worry, you can still deliver the scarcity message nicely. Deliver it with:
- "I really don't want you to miss out," (an attitude of caring for the *client*), rather than

- "You're in the doghouse if you don't come!" (It's all about *our convenience.*)

GET A VERBAL COMMITMENT

Once you've got someone booked in for an appointment, there's something else you can do at the end of the call/visit to increase the likelihood of someone turning up: get a verbal commitment.

Human behaviour is such that we're more likely to do something if we say (out loud) that we're going to do it – it's to do with the cognitive bias of consistency. In simple terms, this bias means we tend to do things consistent with what we've done/said in the past.

With this in mind, the call wrap-up should finish with a question:

> "Ok, John, just confirming that we're going to
> see you at 10am next Tuesday the 20th?"

Then wait for the response.

The mere fact that someone has said out loud that they will attend will make them more likely to attend. Simple.

WHAT ABOUT ONLINE BOOKINGS?

Online bookings are a great convenience for clients. If someone has done their lower back over the weekend (which I have while moving house), then being able to book an appointment when the practice is closed is a real blessing.

However ... what you don't want online bookings to do is to undermine all the good work you've been doing in terms of scarcity, as noted above.

Remember: lack of scarcity = lack of potential commitment = no-shows.

If your book is thrown wide open by your online booking system, then stop it! Now.

Instead, get the best of both worlds. Offer online bookings, BUT only offer a few. The various online booking systems are typically flexible enough that you can set which of your appointments are visible online.

Depending on the size of your practice, I'd suggesting offering 1-2 appointments per day that are visible online. Do NOT, as some practices do, display literally dozens of appointments online that are available in the next week (even if you have holes in your schedule).

Your best strategy for filling (big) holes in your schedule is not making all your empty appointments available online. Instead, use the other practice-growing strategies mentioned in this book.

REMINDERS

Most practices use some kind of reminder system because, let's face it, life can get busy and people forget, even if they know the appointment is important.

The use of text message reminders is simple and reliable but **probably less effective than a phone call**. An automated text is, of course, better than nothing, but can make it too easy for clients to cancel without the opportunity for you to:

(i)   encourage them to keep the appointment, or
(ii)   make another appointment.

On the phone call, the cognitive bias of consistency once again comes into play. If you call someone and ask them to confirm they're attending their appointment and they say, "Yes," they're more likely to come. This is a more likely outcome than if they respond, "Yes," to a faceless text.

A CALL FOR A CANCELLATION IS NOT THE END OF THE STORY

If a client calls to cancel, it's really helpful to understand why they're wanting to cancel. You can say something like:

> "Is everything ok? This appointment is important. Is there a reason you need to cancel it?"

After that, listen to what they have to say.

If a particular event has come up, find out what time the event is and try to make another appointment (while maintaining scarcity). You can even **offer them something sooner** than their original appointment:

> "Sorry to hear you can't make it on Wednesday. Actually, we've had an opportunity come up; are you able to come today?"

It's also okay to ask them to try to attend the appointment. Once again, talk up the importance:

> "Chris is expecting you for this appointment. Are you able to change things so you can still make it?"

If you try this, you'll be surprised how many times a client will change their schedule to make the appointment. If you don't ask, the answer is no.

Finally, if the caller is an existing client, you may be able to **draw on their physio history** to boost the importance of keeping the appointment.

> "Mrs Jones, I notice your records show you've been having an issue with [xyz condition]. We're really keen to ensure that this doesn't get any worse. Is there any way you can keep the appointment so that Chris can make sure you're properly looked after?"

WHAT HAPPENS WHEN THE BEST PLANS FAIL

Sometimes cancellations simply cannot be avoided through extreme circumstances – car crash, extreme weather, funeral etc.

If that's the case, try to rebook the client for another appointment as soon as possible. However, now that you've got a cancellation, you should do whatever you can to fill it – remember, once the time is gone, it's gone.

There are two main ways to fill vacant spots:

- As a general principle, try to offer the first available slot to anyone calling for an appointment. Gaps in your schedule that are sooner are much harder to fill than gaps that are days/weeks away.
- Secondly, get on the phone to try to bring other clients forward to fill the spaces in the schedule. If you know your clients well, you should have a sense of how flexible they are. Nevertheless, you might be surprised by who will agree to come earlier.

Appointment cancellations at a physio practice are a fact of life but with a consistent system in place, they can be minimised. Do anything you can to boost the perceived importance of the appointment, create a feeling of scarcity and get a verbal commitment at the time of booking.

If a client calls to cancel, ask (in a spirit of caring) for the reason for the cancellation and ask to see if they can keep the appointment, stressing the importance. Remember to speak in terms of care for the client rather than about the practice's needs, otherwise you'll come across as rude and uptight.

In all likelihood, you will never completely remove cancellations from your practice, but consistently taking these steps can steadily reduce the numbers and make a huge improvement overall.

13. THE SIMPLE WAY TO HANDLE YOUR MOST TRICKY (YET POTENTIALLY PROFITABLE) CALLERS

For most practices, there are two categories of callers that probably provide more angst than most – one has been around for some time, the other is a relatively new phenomenon to the market place.

The two categories are:
• price shoppers
• preferred-provider seekers.

When someone calls your practice to ask a price-related question, this doesn't necessarily mean that price is an issue for them.

The reason for such calls is because most callers don't really know what else to ask. Technically based businesses experience this kind of call regularly.

I mean, have you ever asked a prospective car repairer what brand of spark plugs they use? Have you asked a firm that services air conditioners the number of particles per million their filters let through? Didn't think so. And the same scenario applies in physiotherapy.

Let's look at price shoppers first.

Price shoppers

When clients ask about price, there are two things you need to include in your discussions to increase call conversion. The first is building rapport.

People deal with businesses they know, like and trust. You want to increase the scores on all counts during this first phone call. This means using the enquirer's name regularly (you'll have to ask) and asking a few questions about them to better understand their needs and show you care.

One thing that can be easy to lose sight of when someone calls to ask about pricing, is they still have an underlying physio need:

- Unless they are a competitor masquerading as a client, the person on the other end of the phone is not really calling you just to find out the price.
- What fundamentally triggered the call was a physio issue – otherwise they would have no reason to call.

This is important to bear in mind when you're answering their price shopping question. However, the tendency is to give a direct answer to a direct question, and in this case, this is a mistake.

What this means is you'll need to basically interrupt their price question to get to the real reason for the call. A simple way of doing so is to say something like, "So I can best help you Steve, I'd like to ask you a few questions first."

You can then ask about the main reason they called you, or about their current concerns.

The second factor is the need to demonstrate value. Price is only a factor if the client views your services as being the same as everyone else – which, of course, they aren't.

No one calls a Ferrari dealership and then quotes the price from a local Kia dealer – these cars are perceived as of different value.

There are a few ways to emphasise the value that your practice offers. The best way is to empathetically uncover the caller's physio concern then advise them how your practice can fix the problem.

Another technique is to differentiate your services by asking questions that highlight the quality of products or services that you offer.

For example, the conversation between your receptionist, Mary, and the client, Brad, might go something like this:

Mary: "So, tell me Brad, what's been going on? What's the problem you're calling about so I understand how we can best help you?"

Brad: "My lower back. I'm not sure what I've done to it, but I can hardly move."

Mary: "Well, I'm really sorry to hear that Brad. The good news is that our physio, Chris, sees lots of people with lower back pain and he's great at getting them fixed up quickly. I assume that's what you want?"

This brief extract of a call with your potential client ticks quite a few boxes:

- Firstly, Mary builds rapport by using Brad's name more than once.
- Secondly, she shows empathy for Brad's condition – you'd be amazed what a difference these two points alone can make.
- Finally, Mary skilfully slips into the conversation that Chris the physio is great at getting Brad's condition fixed quickly. This provides an important point of differentiation if Brad is doing a ring around of multiple physios.

PREFERRED PROVIDER QUERIES

As noted in the introduction, insurers are having a significant impact on the Australian physio community. One of the implications of this phenomenon is clients calling several physios to ask if the physio is a preferred provider for a particular insurer.

This behaviour is no doubt encouraged by the insurers in question. (Some insurers don't run a preferred provider scheme but let clients choose whichever physio they like.) A key part of the message is about saving money for the clients, although it's usually the physios who lose out as they are forced to offer their services for lower prices.

So, if your practice is not a preferred provider for a given insurer then it may appear that this caller is never going to become a client.

However, if you can give the caller a solid reason to choose your (non-preferred) practice over a preferred practice, a portion of callers will choose you. The strategy (similar to price shoppers) is to not directly answer the question straight away but to change the focus of the call.

Specifically, your job is to get the caller to see the value you offer by showing that you:

- care – you can do this by building rapport
- can help their specific situation – you can do this by listening to their concerns and advising how you can help them.

The more you can engage and inform the caller about what you can do for them personally, the better your chances are of keeping them as a client. You can use the same "interrupting" question as before.

When it comes to finally addressing the preferred provider question, you can discuss the payment arrangements for that insurer at your practice.

At Physio Marketing Solutions, we have developed a number of scripts to handle these scenarios. This is because it can often be difficult to remember what to say when the situation arises.

In our experience, pre-prepared scripts increase the chances that:

- you effectively engage the client
- your practice is presented in the best possible light
- ultimately, you maximise the number of calls that you turn into appointments.

STEP THREE: CREATE – STRATEGY

14. INTRODUCTION TO THE *CREATE* PHASE

For some of you, the introduction of the *Create* phase is going to be met with, "At last!"

As tempting as it may be, make sure you do the *Check* and *Count* phases <u>before</u> diving into the *Create* phase. Otherwise, you'll go straight for tactics without an underlying strategy, which would be like stretching first before determining the client's physio concern.

The *Create* phase is divided into three parts. In the introduction, I cover some of the basic strategy in the form of establishing your unique selling point (USP). Then I spend a whole swag of sections looking at each of the marketing tactics you can use. These are divided into two parts: internal and external marketing.

Even with all these sections on tactical marketing activities, the list is not exhaustive. As I identified in the introduction, a key part of a good marketing plan is not just integration but *innovation*.

This means that there can always be other marketing opportunities to slide into your marketing plan.

15. THE ONLY THREE WAYS TO GROW YOUR BUSINESS

When you think about it, there are really only three ways to grow any business:
- increase client numbers
- increase the frequency of their visits
- increase their "basket size" (spend) on each visit.

In this regard, most physios tend to focus on increasing the numbers of new clients – possibly because this is one of the easier things to identify and track.

However, attracting new clients also happens to be the hardest thing to do for most businesses. As noted previously, it's much more expensive to acquire a new client than to serve/nurture an existing one.

In terms of increasing the frequency of visits, this means (in the first instance) maximising the number of clients on your books who visit your practice regularly. Your client retention systems are therefore critical in this regard.

The third technique is about improving basket size or spend on each visit. In my experience, most physios don't have much of a spectrum of pricing – maybe a different price for an initial visit versus subsequent visits, but that's about it.

I think this approach is a mistake. An easy pathway to increasing basket size is to increase your hourly billing rate. There are two basic ways to do this:
- put up your prices
- offer services that are a bit different to routine, and attract a higher price point.

GETTING YOUR PRICING RIGHT

Putting up your prices can be scary to many, but it doesn't have to be.

I've seen many practices agonise about putting up their prices, believing their patients will leave in droves if they do. So, what usually happens when practices put up their prices? Usually, nothing.

Truthfully, your concerns about pricing are really concerns about *value*. We'll come to that in a minute.

First, let me start by saying that you definitely don't want to be the cheapest physio in town.

Being the cheapest practice is often a recipe for a soul-crushing physio practice. With cheap pricing comes "cheap" patients. These are patients who don't value what you do, visit less often than they should, cancel at the last minute, and complain about price etc. Shoot me now!

If you have a heart for serving those of lower socio-economic status, that is certainly laudable, but I'm not convinced that just being cheap is the best way to achieve this.

What would be a much more sustainable business model is to have a sensibly priced, thriving practice that is highly profitable. From there, you can always choose to provide free/discounted services to clients who need them, potentially at a different location.

In recent times, there is a growing trend of such social enterprise businesses that operate on similar models. Indeed, a percentage of all income to Physio Marketing Solutions goes to various charitable organisations, and we do various pro bono marketing work with a similar goal.

If you're not trying to be the cheapest as a strategy for serving the poor, another possible reason for being the cheapest is that you're just getting started. On this basis, perhaps you could offer your services at a lower rate for an initial period, say the first 12 months. Then, as you build your skills, put your prices up.

So, apart from wanting to serve the poor or just getting started as a physio, let's explore the main reason I see practices consciously trying to be the cheapest in their local area. (Some practices just don't realise they're the cheapest.)

I already alluded to it above, but in my experience, if you're aiming to be the cheapest, it's probably because you don't think you provide great *value*.

Despite what we think, price is not the main factor for most people choosing one product over another. If that were the case, Mercedes Benz would never sell a single car, because they're definitely not the cheapest.

The reason Mercedes can charge a lot more for their cars is because of a higher perceived value. There's no reason why you can't do the same in physio.

The simplest way to increase your value (and help you feel more comfortable about charging a higher price) is to take the business class approach that airlines use. This is where they make lots of individual components of their service a bit better. The seats are a bit bigger, the luggage allowance is a bit higher, the food is a bit nicer etc.

If you could implement five to 10 such improvements in your practice (often at little or no additional cost), you'll feel that you are providing a better service and be more confident charging a higher price.

The irony is that in each of the situations, the fundamental service hasn't changed. Both a Mercedes Benz and a Kia both get you from A to B. Similarly, an economy seat and a business class seat both get you from A to B.

By you upping your game with some (relatively minor) improvements, you're still providing the same quality, physio service, yet clients will pay more for it because of the perceived higher value.

As author and clinical psychologist Benjamin Hardy notes in his book *10x is easier than 2x*, creating better results is achieved even by "being 10-20% better (and different) from everyone else."

PRO TIP

- Especially for newer practitioners, there can be a bit of a 'gulp' moment discussing prices. The main reason for that is because they haven't had the chance to see the value that they deliver over an extended period.
- If you gulp/hesitate/flinch when you say a price, patients pick up on it and sense that you may not believe the value of what you're proposing. This leads to less patients taking up your recommendations – if you don't believe it, why would they?
- The simple solution to this is to retrain your brain by practicing saying an amount that is 10X the actual amount. "Mrs Jones, I'm recommending we see you every week for the next 4 weeks where your investment will be $4000" (the real fee is $400). After practicing at 10X, saying the real number seems cheap and great value

---

OFFERING DIFFERENT SERVICES

I'm simultaneously surprised and not surprised that physios don't do more in offering different services.

I'm surprised because hardly anyone does it. I'm also not surprised because hardly anyone does it (fewer role models to copy).

You'll recall the original concept of increasing your hourly rate to grow your business. In my view, one of the best ways to do this is via different services.

To achieve such different services, perception is key. What you're looking for is services that are perceptibly different to standard physio services – and the key word here is "extra."

What are the extra things you can add to standard physio services to create a package of goods that is different to just straight physio?

This can be things like extra testing, extra analysis, extra reporting, extra support, extra resources and so on.

The beauty of this approach is that by offering something that most others aren't doing, you can more or less set your own pricing.

Consider the following example:

> In recent times, I've become a keen runner. When I started to take my running more seriously, my physio offered me a runner's assessment. This involved me running on a treadmill while he videoed me, showed me some screenshots and measurements, then sent me a report with photos/recommendations on how to improve my running.
>
> As a person who has visited the physio many times in my life, this service seemed different. The result was that I saw

the total value of the product as a whole (with all the extra bits) rather than just focusing on price per hour.

There are many opportunities for creating such "products" in physio. The key is to start with a problem, then create a suite of goods that bundle together to address that problem.

In physio, obvious opportunities relate to different body parts such as lower back, neck, knees and elbows, or different interest groups such as cyclists, runners, tradies etc.

From there, the question becomes what extras can you add to the typical physio elements that you would usually offer? Start with your usual physio work, but add extras.

Let's imagine you create a product called "Rapid Runners." Extras could include:

- Extra testing – "We're going to get you to do a series of tests as part of our Rapid Runners assessment."
- Benchmarking – "Let's see how your results compare to other people who've done the Rapid Runners test."
- Photos/video/scans – "This will show you areas to improve if you want to get a better Rapid Runners score."
- Reporting – "You'll get a seven-page report comprising the most recent research in this area, your Rapid Runner results, the benchmarks and clear recommendations for your next steps."
- Resources – "Included in this product is exclusive access to our Rapid Runner training videos, helping you to learn more about improving your Rapid Runner score."
- Branded items that support the package – You could include exclusive Rapid Runners stickers, fridge magnets, key rings etc that include the brand and the key messages from the program.
- Physical goods – You could include branded physio-related devices such as a Rapid Runners band, ball etc plus a

branded Rapid Runners folder for literature, test results, the report, branded stickers.

Let's be clear what I'm talking about here and what I'm not. This is not selling snake oil. Any extras that you include must be underpinned by sound physio advice.

But the truth is for many clients, they *want* more from you and if you can put together an attractive package that meets their needs, well, why not?

I was really happy to get the runners assessment from my physio, and it didn't stop me visiting the physio for treatment or further advice.

In the book *80/20 Sales and Marketing*, author Perry Marshall notes that the "80/20 (rule) says that 20 percent of the people will spend four times the money."

Why not be the physio who attracts the top 20% (who, according to Marshall, spend four times the money) by offering different products?

A final step to creating your different service is giving it a unique name.

Interestingly, research shows that the use of either alliteration or rhyming words generate higher levels of trust and in turn, a higher perceived value.

For alliteration, you could have something like Rapid Runner or Back Builders, or rhyming names like Hello Elbow, Neck in Check.

To make it easier to promote this extra service, train the whole team on what's included so that the person answering the phone can say to callers:

- "Sorry to hear you're suffering with what sounds like chronic lower back pain. We have a special program called 'Back Builders' which sounds perfect for what you need.
- It includes 3 easy strength and flexibility tests, 1 hour's custom treatment from our highly experienced physios, a benchmarked report against people of your age, and a video series to build your knowledge at home. Your investment is $xxx and it's very been popular with our clients. Would you like to book that in?"

16. BECOME A CLIENT MAGNET BY DEFINING YOUR UNIQUE SELLING POINT (USP)

As we now move to the *Create* phase of the process, it's important to be really clear about what your practice stands for and the broad offer you make to the marketplace.

If you think you're "just another physio," that's how the market will treat you. And in the current competitive environment, you cannot afford to do that.

As a case in point, I recently looked through the Yellow Pages listing for a client in a regional area. Among the dozen or so physios in that area who had paid for a bigger listing in Yellow Pages online, NOT ONE of them stood out. At least, not for the right reasons!

All of them focused on either:
- fairly generic physio elements that clients would <u>expect</u> from physios – technical skills, friendly staff etc, or
- things that clients don't value much, if at all – e.g. family-owned business.

The best way to help you stand out from the market place and become a client magnet is to define your USP.

A USP is something that sets your practice apart from your competitors. However, a quick scan of physio websites reveals a lot of very similar claims. "We're friendly, our team is well trained, we're passionate about physiotherapy," etc.

This is good and bad. The bad news is that most physio practices offering this fairly generic USP are not getting the benefit of differentiating themselves from other physios in the marketplace.

The good news is that with so few physios genuinely offering any kind of meaningful USP, it makes it easier for your practice to stand out.

As you consider your USP, just be sure to avoid the meaningless claims that most other physios are making.

Apart from the fact that most physio's claims are fairly generic, they're also difficult for clients to quantify – and remember, as prospective new clients, they're looking at your claims through sceptical eyes.

Being friendly and technically cannot be independently verified – there's no friendliness benchmark, no independent standard for technical skills (beyond the minimum qualifications that every physio has). As a result, these claims are effectively discounted by potential clients.

> When you claim that your practice is friendly, technically skilled and passionate about physiotherapy, what your prospective clients hear is, "Blah, blah, blah."

Apart from these claims being generic, they also fail to recognise that **what clients are really buying is a result**. It's like clients are silently saying to themselves after hearing each claim, "So what? What difference does that make to me?"

At their most basic, there are really only a few benefits that a client (of any type) gets from any transaction:
- look good
- feel good
- make/save money
- save time.

Whether you buy a meal at a restaurant, get a haircut or have your car serviced, you are achieving one or more of the above benefits.

With these factors in mind, your job is to create a USP that quantifies the unique, measurable outcome that the client gets from dealing with you, in a way that is hard for your competitors to match.

IDENTIFY YOUR BIGGEST BENEFITS

Think about the three biggest benefits your practice provides. In doing so, explain WHY those benefits are important to your clients. Think in terms of what your business does for your client and the end result they desire from dealing with you.

BE UNIQUE

Your USP separates you from the competition – if you're offering the same as everyone else, why would they choose you?

Your USP helps your clients decide that your practice is a preferred, more desirable choice. Also, be aware that being unique for the sake of it is only valuable if your clients value that uniqueness.

I'm pretty sure there aren't too many practices out there doing physiotherapy while hopping on one leg. While this is definitely a unique claim, it seems highly unlikely your clients would value this unique (and slightly bizarre) difference.

Your USP needs to be written in such a way that it creates desire and urgency. Your USP can be stated three ways – product, offer or guarantee:
- PRODUCT: "A cutting-edge healing protocol that will have you back on your feet in no time."
- OFFER: "Get rid of back pain in just three sessions."
- GUARANTEE: "If you don't experience a substantial improve with your neck pain in 30 days, we'll keep working on you at no cost."

<u>Solve a pain point or "performance gap" that is common in your industry</u>

Identify which needs are going unfulfilled in either your industry or your local market. The need or gap that exists between the current situation and the desired objective is known as a "performance gap." Businesses that base their USP on an industry performance gap have an immediate advantage.

Some examples of business USPs include "Pizza delivered in 30 minutes or it's free," (Dominos) or "15 minutes could save you 15% or more," (car insurer). You can see how they touch a pain point – "I'm hungry and don't want to wait," and "I want to save money on insurance but don't want to have to wait on the phone."

So, what are the most frustrating things your clients experience when working with you or your industry? What are the things you hear in social situations that people say about dealing with physios? Alleviate that "PAIN," and describe how in your USP.

BE SPECIFIC AND OFFER PROOF

Consumers are often sceptical of advertising claims. Overcome their scepticism by being specific and offering proof when possible, remembering Australian law prohibits clinical testimonials for physios. Here's an example:
- Pain – Many people don't like to go to the physio because they don't run on time.
- USP – "We guarantee that your appointment will start within 10 minutes of your appointment time, or we'll take $50 off your bill."

CREATE THE OFFER AND MAKE IT CLEAR

The most powerful USPs are so perfectly written, you cannot change or move even a single word. After you write your USP, it should easily flow into your various advertising activities.

Through our work with various clients, we've created a number of unique USPs that make it easy for clients to identify why they should deal with the practice. These have included getting a particular service outcome, having a guaranteed service standard, and accessing a unique offer.

Not only did these USPs make these practices more attractive to their potential clients (the USPs feature on their websites), they have a second purpose. The USPs underpin all the other marketing activities by the practices, making an integrated approach to their marketing easier.

If creating your USP seems all too hard (there is a skill in putting together a USP), visit **www.physiotherapymarketing.com** and send us a note to get some professional help.

STEP FOUR: CREATE – INTERNAL MARKETING

17. INTRODUCTION TO *INTERNAL MARKETING*

The first part of the *Create* process is internal marketing. This is marketing to your existing clients.

As the infographic below shows, all clients are not created equal. Internal marketing (to existing clients) is an excellent place to start your marketing.

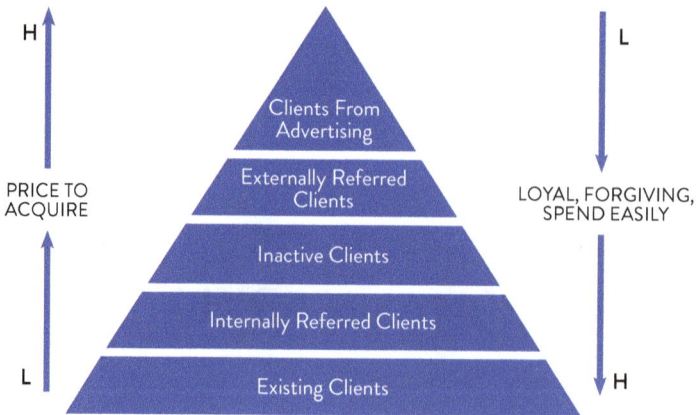

H

L

PRICE TO
ACQUIRE

LOYAL, FORGIVING,
SPEND EASILY

Clients From
Advertising

Externally Referred
Clients

Inactive Clients

Internally Referred Clients

Existing Clients

L

H

18. NOW THAT YOU KNOW YOUR ACV, HOW DO YOU GROW IT?

By definition, the only way to grow your ACV (average client value) is to get your clients spending more with you.

To achieve this goal, you're going to need them to take advantage of more of the services you offer.

For example, imagine that you work heavily with athletes, yet currently only 1% of your clients take advantage of your video running analysis. However, because of some internal promotions, you increase this number to 15%. Let's see what effect this would have on your ACV.

To make the calculations simple, we'll assume the following:
* active client database: 1000 clients
* average client value: $400/patient/year
* cost of video running analysis: $300
* current level of clients undertaking video running analysis annually: less than1%
* level of clients undertaking video running analysis after an internal promotion: 15%

The change:
* practice ACV before the promotion: $400
* practice ACV after the promotion: $445

For the mathematically inclined, in the 'before' example, total practice revenue was $400,000 from 1000 clients: an ACV of $400. In the 'after' example, 150 clients undertook the extra $300 video running analysis, adding an extra $45,000 income. Total practice revenue was therefore $445,000 from 1000 clients: an ACV of $445

Now that we know how much ACV can be increased by one marketing activity, we now turn our minds to how to improve ACV. Fortunately, to do so, it's simply a matter of using the internal marketing techniques listed below to improve your engagement with your existing clients.

"PRODUCTISING" YOUR SERVICES

I mentioned above that adding extra elements to your existing services can allow you to offer more value and in turn, charge more.

It's also a great way to differentiate what you do from every other physio in town who almost certainly isn't doing this. This means if people are shopping around for different physio services, more of them will end up as your clients.

To figure out which of these personalised products you should create, simply look at your practice data. Which services are you offering more regularly; which client groups are you already serving at an above average rate?

Bottom line: if you implement even one or two of these packages, you can increase your ACV quite markedly.

19. EMAIL MARKETING – THE MONEY IS IN THE LIST

For some of you reading this, even the *idea* of marketing to your clients by email will be met with an audible gasp. Yet, email marketing can be an incredibly effective way of promoting your service to your clients.

Before we get into the specifics of how to do email marketing, I need to address with you the most common objections I hear in this space.

No one reads emails these days

This is simply not true. While the level of email that we get has certainly increased, email nevertheless is a very useful form of marketing – if it's done right.

In my own business, I have gained numerous new clients simply from sending emails, and my target market is much smaller than yours.

In direct marketing circles, where the client value can make or break the business, there is a saying:

The money is in the list.

This statement reflects the fact that the more people you have who receive an email from you, the more likely you are to be able to sell what you're promoting. It's a numbers game.

While a return of 2-3% may not sound like much, if you have a list of 1000 people, that's 20-30 people who will take on the service you're offering. Of course, if your list is 10,000 people then that's 200-300 new clients.

It's true that not everyone will read your emails, but some of your clients will. And if what you're offering them is applicable to their needs, you might just have made another sale.

I don't want to appear too spammy

Firstly, let's be clear. I'm not suggesting you email your clients every day or every week. The list of services that you offer is finite, so you could run out of content and relevance pretty quickly.

However, sending something out once or twice a month should present no problem. For any clients who are not wanting to receive what you're sending out, you should have an easy "unsubscribe" option for them.

I don't want to appear too salesy

Let's talk about sales because I feel that a lot of physios reel at the thought without really thinking it through. Here's a harsh reality:

> Stop selling (anything) and you're out of business.

So, some level of sales is absolutely essential.

What physios are nervous about, however, is coming across as salesy. To address this, I need to tell you a little story.

Some time before setting up Physio Marketing Solutions, I was a sales manager working for a large corporate, where my team was selling about $25 million worth of products each year. I had a dozen people reporting to me.

As you might imagine, in a sales organisation, we kept a very close eye on the numbers – how many sales each person was making. Among my team members, I had one sales rock star, Jodie. A couple of years in a row, she was the highest seller nationally, by quite some way.

You could be forgiven for thinking that, therefore, she must have been a really pushy sales type. She wasn't.

Sure, she was focused on the task at hand, but the one area that separated her from the other sales people was something that might surprise you. She focused very heavily on the client's needs. I'll repeat those last few words again for emphasis – the *client's* needs.

If a sales person is doing a good job, you won't feel like you're being sold to – AT ALL.

Poor sales people will push *their* agenda. This is where sales gets a bad reputation. The stereotypical used-car sales person gets that reputation because they are trying very hard to convince you to do something you don't want to do.

In a physio context, if you are genuinely coming across as (i) helping your clients' mobility (ii) getting them out of pain, and/or (iii) giving them peace of mind about an aspect of their health, then there really is no issue. As a consumer, who *wouldn't* want those things?

So, now that we've looked at the objections, let's look at the how-to aspects. With your email marketing, as you're writing, do your best to look through your clients' eyes – think about your avatar (see section 8).

The mistake I see with such marketing communication is that it focuses too heavily on the technical aspects of what you're offering, rather than the result.

Imagine you're promoting better balance for elderly patients. Clients have an interest in some of the technical aspects – such as how long the process takes and how difficult it will be.

But apart from that, clients generally don't care about the specifics of the process – all they want is a great result when they're done. They want to feel better about themselves, more confident on their feet, more stable and so on.

One other element of email marketing to consider is the use of video. Just because you're sending an email doesn't mean it needs to be boring.

To spice it up, you can embed a video. Video is a very powerful marketing tool and with more and more smartphones about, the consumption of video content is at an all-time high.

For your videos within an email, keep them interesting and focus on the outcomes for the clients. A bit of entertainment doesn't hurt either – a growing trend is so-called "infotainment," a mix of information and entertainment.

To get your email marketing on autopilot, pre-plan your content, otherwise it probably won't happen. With a bit of imagination, it's not too hard to plan a 12-month email program for clients that takes advantage of different treatments at different times of the year to maximise the return.

Each time you send out an email for a physio practice, you can bring in additional business, as long as the messaging represents the receiver's interests and needs. Given that this marketing is by email (at no cost), you don't need many additional appointments booked to make it well worth its while.

20. CLIENT LOUNGE MARKETING

One of the things I love about my business is getting to visit a lot of different physio practices. I'd say I've seen just about every type including:

- rat holes that I wouldn't send my worst enemies to
- practices with a spa-like vibe that would be entirely appropriate for a ladies' full day pampering session, and
- just about everything in between.

So, when I raise the topic of client lounge marketing (I don't like the term "waiting room," given the emphasis on *waiting*), I recognise that this experience in physio land can be highly variable.

In simple terms, *client lounge marketing* is about raising awareness for something. This could be a new or existing service, it could be a disease-state that clients need to look out for, or it could be highlighting your client referral system.

What I'm not talking about is a collection of tatty posters, haphazardly attached to your walls. This approach, in my view, gives the impression of practice chaos.

The best client lounge marketing I've seen, by a country mile, is presented on TV screens. Many practices have TVs, and these can be used very effectively to market to your clients without detracting from the overall aura of the lounge.

Some practices have their own messages on the TV screens, which vary in quality. The main mistake I see, apart from pretty ordinary looking graphics, is (once again) a focus on the technology or technique, rather than the outcome for the clients.

Whatever you do, do NOT have a TV showing the news. Here are the facts:

- bad news sells more than good news
- news services typically run at about a 70/30 bad/good news ratio (sometimes as high as 90/10).

If you want your client to invest in your services, agree to a treatment plan, or take up one of your tailored programs, showing them a whole bunch of bad news before their appointment is a *really* bad idea.

By all means entertain them if they have a short wait, but show them something educational or positive, rather than doom and gloom via the mainstream media.

If you're wondering where to start with your client lounge, what I recommend you do is go for a walk and imagine yourself as a new client. Then come back to the practice and pay close attention to everything that a new client would see.

You might be surprised what marketing and other messages your clients are getting when they come to visit, especially for the first time. Failing that, get a straight-talking friend to do the same thing and get their feedback.

21. BECOME A WALKING BILLBOARD FOR YOUR PRACTICE WITHOUT SAYING A WORD

When I was a kid, I really enjoyed watching comedy shows on TV. One of my favourite shows (that my parents allowed me to watch), was on the ABC and was called "Australia, you're standing in it."

One of the regular skits on the show involved a woman in a fashion shop. She had a passion for hot pants (among other things) and her signature phrase was, "If you've got it, show it!"

The comedy, of course, was that her taste in fashion was terrible and no, she didn't actually "have it."

Anyway, this same principle – if you've got it, show it – can be applied to your practice. Fortunately, that doesn't involve wearing hot pants!

But what it does involve is (tastefully) using what you wear as a silent, walking billboard, for your practice.

Ever walked into a shop where all the staff are wearing a badge promoting something that they're doing. "Want a new xyz? Ask me how." The reason they do this is because these promotions work.

At one point in my career, I worked in the pharmacy industry and I had a chance to talk to a brand manager from a very well-known over-the-counter medication.

One of the techniques they used in certain pharmacies was to get all the staff to wear the same shirt on a Friday. The shirt had an embroidered message which mentioned the brand name of the product.

The outcome? That product increased in sales EVERY DAY the staff wore the shirts.

I've yet to see the branded shirt idea in physiotherapy but I can't think of a sensible reason why practices wouldn't do this.

Importantly, whether it's a shirt or a badge, this kind of promotion can be done *tastefully*. I understand, given that you're offering professional services, you don't want to come across as doing anything gaudy or cheesy. But the outcomes are well worth the effort.

For example, if you decided you wanted to use the new year to promote a flexibility program, you could get a set of badges for less than a hundred dollars with a simple message like:

"Best flexibility of your life? Ask me how."

If the idea of badges is not your thing, what about getting a similar (shorter) message embroidered on a set of shirts:

"New Year! Better Back!" or

"Stable Seniors. Stupendous!"

Your team could all wear these on a given day/days of the week. The important part is to have something sufficiently intriguing for a client to ask about it.

Under the scenario above, you'd be up for perhaps $60-$80 per shirt (including embroidery).

Even if these shirts were just limited to the reception staff, how many extra treatments/referrals would you need to sell to cover your investment of a few hundred dollars? About one.

And you could run the promotion a few times a year.

22. UPSELLING – MAKING IT EASIER FOR CLIENTS TO BUY MORE FROM YOU

Just when you thought I'd already pushed the marketing envelope to breaking point, I'm now going to talk about upselling.

Upselling is simply offering clients additional products/services. Made famous by McDonald's "Would you like fries with that?" upselling can have a dramatic effect on total sales. Data I've seen suggests that McDonald's six-word question has a 30% uptake and a 5-10% increase in total spend.

For the sake of a question that takes one or two seconds to ask, McDonald's increased the purchase by around 20% for three out of each 10 clients they serve. Who *wouldn't* be happy with that kind of uplift in turnover, purely because of asking a question that takes two seconds?

Of course, a physio practice is not McDonald's. The expectations are different and upselling needs to be tackled in a different way, but the results can still be significant. Yet, most practices just don't do it – or if they do, they don't do it consistently.

Before you write off the concept altogether, consider the following discussion between friends Beryl and Betty:

> Beryl: "So, what have you been up to lately, Betty?"

> Betty: "Well, doing some work to get me walking better."

> Beryl: "Yeah, I noticed. You look to be moving a lot better."

> Betty: "Thanks. My physio has been promoting a 'Summer Stable Seniors' program."

Beryl: "Wow, I should get that done too. So, who's your physio?"

Betty: "ABC Physio."

Beryl: "ABC Physio?"

Betty: "Yes, why do you ask?"

Beryl: "Because I'm a client of theirs too; they never asked ME about that!"

Often, we look at upselling to clients as though we're asking them to do something they don't want to do. However, for many of your clients, the reality is they might be upset about NOT being asked – as demonstrated in the Beryl and Betty example above.

The words and the delivery are critical. With a well-crafted sentence delivered in a relaxed, caring manner, an upsell can feel as natural as offering a house visitor a cup of tea.

For example, when a client is attending the counter for an appointment, reception staff can simply ask the client if they've heard about whatever program the practice is running.

This is such a non-threatening question to ask, doesn't feel salesy and can have a very positive outcome. The *worst* thing a client is likely to say to that question is, "No, it's all right," or "No, not interested."

However, the most likely thing a client will say is, "No, what is it?"

Of course, if you don't have, for example, a Summer Stable Seniors program, you can always create one. This sort of program is best done as part of an integrated and innovative marketing campaign.

23. TOTAL RECALL – TERMINATING INFREQUENT CLIENT VISITS

As part of your efforts to maximise your ACV, client visit frequency is absolutely critical.

Another industry that is heavily dependent on an effective recall system is hairdressing. During a recent challenging economic time, when clients were looking to minimise their spending, one thing that occurred was clients stretching out their visits to get their hair done.

Over the course of a year, this resulted in a 20% reduction in total sales.

When you consider that most businesses have significant fixed costs (regardless of whether they see one client a day or 20), this kind of reduction had a dramatic impact on profit for these hairdressers.

This same phenomenon is also true for physios. Consider the financial cost of an increase or reduction in your client visit frequency as follows:

ASSUMPTIONS
- A practice has a static 1000 active clients across the year.
- The average spend on each visit is $100.

Average visits/client per annum	Total income per annum
2.5	$250,000
3.0	$300,000
3.5	$350,000
4.0	$400,000

As you can see, the implications are enormous for improving this figure and justify some extra effort and attention. But this requires a delicate balance.

For many physio clients, they typically only visit following a fall/injury or flare-up of a chronic condition.

Some physio practices tend to increase the number of patient appointments even though the patient could be helped to overcome their ailment in a shorter time. In my view, this is short-term thinking.

It's much better to develop the reputation as a practice that gets people back on their feet quickly, rather than clients dreading attending because they know they'll be asked back for numerous appointments.

Putting aside that philosophical challenge, what is important is to minimise cancellations and no-shows.

As noted in Step Two, building a sense of importance for the appointment is a great way of ensuring clients actually turn up.

Be careful not to emphasise the reminder system at the time of making subsequent appointments as this can undermine the "importance/scarcity" message. i.e. If something were really important, there wouldn't be such a big need to make the reminder – the client would be more likely to remember it themselves.

As part of the process, keep a close eye on the recall rates you're achieving and be prepared to ramp up your system if you're not getting the results you're looking for. The numbers above show it's worth the effort.

24. LAPSED CLIENTS – UNLOCKING THE GOLD IN YOUR PRACTICE

With any physio practice, at any given moment, there is always a number of "lapsed" clients. These are either clients who have:

- missed their last appointment, or
- been recommended a treatment plan or special service but have not proceeded with the treatment.

The reality is this group (particularly the latter) represents a significant and valuable opportunity for practices. As the saying goes, "There's gold in them hills." In this case, there's gold in them lapsed clients!

From a marketing point of view, there are a few ways to unlock this gold and the process is pretty simple:

- The first step is to run a report from your practice management system to identify the clients who fall into either of the above categories. If you're not sure how to do so, contact your software provider for advice.
- The second step, now that you have the list, is to allocate a team member to get in touch with the clients.

If it seems that this would be difficult to fit into the daily schedule, you could do a lot worse than paying someone specifically to contact these lapsed clients. The potential value in doing so would way outweigh the moderate costs of the extra assistance.

Your options for contacting these clients include phone, email or mail. I would suggest contacting the lapsed clients in that order. In terms of the message that you provide to these clients, there are a couple of things to emphasise:

- Keeping on top of your health is important – we want to help you stay pain-free for years to come.

- If the client has a physio condition that requires a treatment plan, delaying the treatment is not going to make it better and may make it worse.

Particularly over the phone, the tone of the delivery of these messages is really important. An old boss of mine used to tell me, "Say it in sorrow, not in anger."

Lapsed clients are far less likely to respond to a wagging finger (or parental tone) than contact from the practice that shows care for them and their health.

25. THE NUMBER ONE WAY TO BOOST CLIENT NUMBERS AT YOUR PRACTICE

Data from numerous sources points to the fact that, hands-down, the most effective way to boost client numbers in most businesses is via referred clients. While this happens to a certain extent without your involvement, even better is to have an *active* client referral system.

Client referrals have a lot going for them. Good clients tend to associate with other good clients. Referred clients are generally easier to deal with and are more trusting of your business (because of the referral).

This also means, where applicable, referred clients are more likely to accept treatment plans and are less likely to quibble over price.

Before we discuss this matter further, a little disclaimer is needed. In section 3, I talked about regulatory restrictions on physio practices. Some physios I've spoken to have indicated that having a client referral system that offers a reward for referring clients is frowned on by AHPRA.

AHPRA has apparently written to some physios telling them to stop running such a system (advertising a client referral system on your website is not a good idea).

So, in this situation, you have three choices:
- Do nothing – this is a really bad idea. Presumably, you're reading this book because you want to boost your business. Not having any kind of client referral system in place is leaving so much business on the table, it's doesn't bear thinking about.
- Adopt a "positive reinforcement" system. This system doesn't appear to breach AHPRA guidelines. Under this

scenario, you routinely thank clients who refer other clients to the practice. This can be sending a card/letter and a gift/voucher *after* the referral. Basically, the more positive an experience someone has with referring a client to you, the more likely they are to do it again.

- <u>Create an active rewards system.</u> If you're going to adopt this approach, this needs to be a private communication with your clients and not something to publish on your website. If you're wrestling with this model, there are a couple of things to bear in mind that can appease any apparent conflicts with the AHPRA guidelines:
  - o This approach is consistent with the policy intention of AHPRA guidelines about avoiding encouraging *unnecessary* medical attention. While AHPRA may not publicly acknowledge this, as physios you know Australians need (basic) physio care.
  - o Secondly, it is very unlikely you'll be called into question given its private nature (direct to clients).

If you're going to adopt an active rewards system, you'll need to offer some sort of incentive for clients who refer others to your practice. For example, the system could involve entering referring clients into a draw to win something each time they refer someone new.

I suggest avoiding physio prizes (especially discounts on services) as these can come across as self-serving. Holidays, petrol vouchers and gift cards are popular but seasonal prizes can work well too, e.g. Christmas hampers, Easter baskets etc.

One other thing to bear in mind is the issue of government permits. Rules for competitions vary from state to state. In some states, no permits are needed. In other states, you may need to apply for a permit, or run the competition in a particular way to get around that need.

One distinction in many states' laws relate to games of skill versus games of chance.

If you can include a skill element, you often won't need a permit. The best way to do this is adding something like 'tell us in 25 words or less what you like most about this practice'. Then it becomes a game of skill where the best answer wins (game of skill) rather than a lucky draw (game of chance).

Another way to recognise clients who refer others to your practice is to hold a client appreciation event. You need no special agenda for the event other than to say thank you to your best clients. Hold it in-house or go out, do it annually or as often as you like.

From a financial point of view, each new client for your business is likely to spend (based on data from clients of Physio Marketing Solutions) in the order of $300-$500 in the first year. And the same in year two, year three etc.

It is not surprising then, that at Physio Marketing Solutions, the client referral systems we run with our clients have been some of our most effective marketing tools.

STEP FIVE: CREATE – EXTERNAL MARKETING

26. INTRODUCTION TO *EXTERNAL MARKETING*

Even with the best internal systems in place, there are times when you're going to need to go to the market to attract new clients. While such clients are more expensive to acquire (as noted in the infographic below, repeated from section 17), sometimes this simply can't be helped.

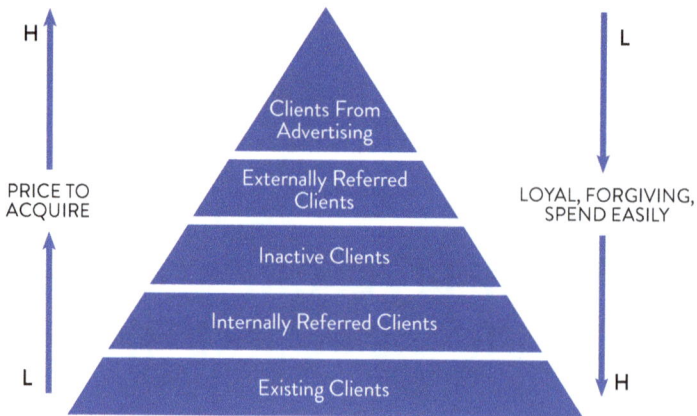

In my experience, the best marketing systems are a "chair with many legs," i.e. you run many marketing sources simultaneously so that if one leg disappears, your chair won't fall over. External marketing is an important part of this system.

Further, the reality is, if your business is new, relying on internal marketing alone is not going to generate sufficient results. This is particularly true for a business like physiotherapy, where most clients only visit you when something goes wrong.

27. BUILDING A WEBSITE THAT TURNS BROWSERS INTO BUYERS

Physio websites are as common as fleas on an untreated dog. It would be rare to find a physio practice these days that doesn't have some kind of website. Plus, clients *expect* you to have one.

However, having a website for your practice and having one that turns browsers into buyers are two very different stories.

Have you ever thought about what the fundamental purpose of a website is? Most practices, from what I can tell, put up what is basically an online brochure. i.e. This is who we are and what we do.

Having that kind of presence will no doubt generate some new clients for you – though the quality of your SEO is a factor – but often this kind of website doesn't really address the website's goal.

At a live event recently, I asked the audience what they thought the purpose of a website was and answers I got included that the website is there to inform and provide information about the services you offer.

However, from my point of view, **the website is about getting people to make an appointment**. Plain and simple.

Information is all well and good but if someone doesn't make an appointment as a result of the information, you've wasted your time.

So how do you build a website that turns browsers into buyers? There are a few key things the website needs to do:
- Answer three questions in about five seconds
- Generate an emotional response
- Make it obvious what the next step is.

THREE QUESTIONS

It is well documented that attention spans are getting shorter and shorter. Social media definitely hasn't helped – ever sat and watched someone flicking through Facebook/Instagram? You'll see what I mean.

In terms of websites, different studies have tested how long you've got to engage someone when they get to your website before they click off somewhere else. Results I've seen vary between about three and seven seconds. For the purpose of this exercise, we'll choose five seconds as our target attention span.

And while our attention spans are becoming shorter, the volume of material we come across on a daily basis is becoming greater and greater. This means we've got to work even harder to get people's attention.

Therefore, in the five seconds, your website has to answer three questions:

1. What's this about?

You know what it's like. You've stumbled across a website and you spend the first few moments thinking, "What is this?"

I have seen physio websites where it's not even obvious that it's a physio – one even had a whole bunch of trees on the home page (and very little text)! Resist the urge to be too cute on your website, and make sure it's really clear that you're a physio practice.

2. Who is this for?

Clients don't generally travel too far to go the physio unless you're offering something unusual. So, in physiotherapy, you can answer this question by being very clear about *where you are*. How often have you landed on a webpage only to discover that it was in a different part of town/city/state/country? Make it really clear where your practice is.

3. Why should I engage?

In my experience, most physios do okay with questions one and two (though there's room for improvement for some). However, the question most often missed by physios is, "Why should I engage?"

Fewer than one in a hundred would answer this question well. Part of the reason for this is because it requires some real creativity and thought.

If physios do address this question, they tend to answer it with things that clients don't really value. This includes generic claims about being friendly, technically competent and passionate about physio. I've heard it described as "tickets to the dance." Ie. You get to go to the dance, but that's about it

If you weren't friendly, technically competent and passionate about physiotherapy, **no one would go to you!** What you want is a unique benefit for the client in dealing with you. In this regard, the section above on USPs (section 16) can help.

GENERATE AN EMOTIONAL RESPONSE

As scientists, most physios assume that most of our decision-making is on the basis of facts and figures, rather than emotions. All very left brain. However, the reality is, as objective as we think we are, our emotions are always at play and the experts tell us that we make decisions based on emotion and justify on logic.

Don't believe me? How would you react if a rep you've never met turns up to your practice for an appointment wearing an orange suit? Even though they may have a sound understanding of their products and how they can help you, the colour of their suit affects how you feel about them.

For some of you, the orange suit will immediately make you feel like this person can't possibly know what they're talking about. For some of you, the orange suit will make you feel that perhaps they are representing technology that is new, exciting or even a bit edgy.

As more evidence, what if their suit were pink, white, bright red? None of those things fundamentally change the help they can give you, but it's inevitable that we would have some kind of emotional reaction.

In this regard, a question for you to ask yourself is, "What emotion do you want someone landing on your website to feel?" Do you want them to feel inspired, excited, calm, comfortable, loved, or cared for?

The photos, design and even fonts on your website will give this message to your prospective clients very quickly (and subconsciously).

PHOTOS

It is a fact that the human eye is drawn to human faces – even from when we're babies. A casual glance at a magazine stand will demonstrate that this point is not lost on magazine producers, whose success is dependent on split-second decisions whether to buy their magazine or not.

When designing your website, take advantage of this fact.

Even though you're in the business of physiotherapy, do NOT have the main image at the top of your homepage as a treatment table – yes, I've seen this on physio websites. Stop it. Bad dog!

Instead, you want smiling faces and even better, actual shots from your practice. Stock photos are okay, but for a few hundred dollars you can get a one-hour photo shoot with a professional photographer that will give you all the pictures you need.

You'll need candid shots with a "client," group photos, individual photos and some practice shots.

> ### PRO TIP
>
> - Given the attention-grabbing properties of human faces, your "money shot" for the top of your website should be a happy, smiling client/avatar (refer Section 8) interacting with your team. Subconsciously, you want people to imagine themselves being in your practice, having that same happy experience.

MAKE IT OBVIOUS WHAT THE NEXT STEP IS

If you've done a good job answering the three questions in five seconds and generating a suitable emotional response, you've effectively got permission to engage the potential client. This means they're likely to spend longer on your website to find out more information.

However, as I've discussed, giving them more information is only part of the process and certainly not the final step.

Many practice websites do not make it really clear what the visitor should do next. Do you want them to fill in a form, email you, call you? Whatever it is, make it really clear (more than once) and give them a reason to act.

OTHER TIPS

The perfect home page for your website is pretty much the holy grail. Looking at "traffic" data (how many visitors each page of the website gets), I've seen a physio website where **85% of visitors never go beyond the home page**. Eighty five percent!

The crux here is to get a highly functioning home page, so put all of your effort into getting that right, even if it is to the detriment of other pages.

An extra note for physios: I know you guys really love your technology and the range of treatments you offer, but please don't make your website for physios, make it for clients.

Your time and energy are limited, so aim to get the best bang for your buck. Physios who I deal with often agonise over a page about a particular treatment and then are disappointed to discover that such pages may be lucky to get one or two views per month.

28. THE LARGE POOL OF "WARMED UP" POTENTIAL CLIENTS JUST WAITING FOR YOU

As we move our way through the different categories in the new client sources pyramid, here's something you mightn't have thought of:

Some other (non-competing) business
already has a relationship with your desired clients.

This bears repeating. There is almost certainly a number of businesses near you that have built a trusting relationship with your perfect prospective clients. As you'll appreciate, getting to this trusting status with a client is a major hurdle for businesses.

So, why not take advantage of this?

The answer is approaching local businesses to establish referrals and joint promotions – this can be really beneficial for both sides.

There are a range of businesses that you can approach in this regard but those that have a "health" aspect to them are a good place to start. Examples include:

- other health care professionals (particularly doctors)
- gyms, massage therapists, Pilates or yoga instructors
- local sports teams.

Ideally, you want to establish a situation where you both promote each other's business. Alternatively, you may offer a personal reward (free treatment) to a business owner once they've referred a certain number of clients.

When you are thinking about offering the promotion of another business to your clients, it's easy enough to present as:

"At XYZ physio, we care about your total health. So, we've teamed up with ABC business to offer you a *free hearing/eye check, discount of service,*" etc.

From a client's point of view, this comes across as caring rather than salesy.

You may find the prospect of approaching local businesses daunting. Here are a few tips to make the process easier:
- Introduce yourself as a "neighbour" as quickly as possible. A number of these businesses are quite used to being "pitched" by a plethora of sales people. The sooner you can identify yourself as a neighbour, the sooner their guard will come down.
- Ask to see the relevant manager and check if they've got a few minutes. You want to be talking to the right person at a time when they can see you. If need be, make an appointment to come back and see them.
- Enter the discussions with an open, inquisitive mind and find out what you can do to help them, rather than just focusing on what you want. My experience is when you ask such questions, surprising things can turn up:
  - o Visiting a gym with a client, we introduced ourselves as neighbours. As luck would have it, the owner had just had a cancelled appointment, so we got to spend a few minutes with her.
  - o After a brief discussion about business and the neighbourhood, I said, "It occurs to me that we've probably got the potential for sharing customers with each other. How can we help you?"
  - o The principal said, "Well, we have a team meeting of our 10 personal trainers next month and I'd really like it if you could come and do a talk for us." Did you get

that? Ten personal trainers! Going and doing a 30 minute talk for that gym was a no-brainer, particularly with the potential for 10 trainers referring new clients.

- In the event that the other business has no idea what they want or how you could help each other, it pays to have a few options up your sleeve such as:
  - o promoting each other in your newsletters
  - o preparing tailored brochures you can swap to give to your clients on behalf of the other business, e.g. common injuries at the gym and what to do first
  - o setting up a special offer for referred clients – price discount, bundling, bulk buys etc.

Whatever arrangements you come up with, expect to have to visit the local business several times to make things happen. It's very rare for a system to be established after just one visit.

Similarly, do what you can to achieve a good launch. Whatever system you come up with that allows you to refer clients to the other business, get it happening as soon as you can. If the other business sees that they're receiving clients from the arrangement, they're more likely to be engaged in ensuring it continues.

There are other ways to engage with local businesses for mutual benefit such as partnering with local restaurants.

The first step is to approach a local restaurant and mention you've got a scheme to help them get more business. Always start with what's in it for them, not you.

The idea is to get a voucher for a free dessert (or similar) for you to send to your clients on their birthday. For the restaurant, this is a negligible financial risk because clients are:

- unlikely to go out for their birthday by themselves – this means they'll be accompanied by other paying guests

- likely to order at least tea or coffee with their free dessert and possibly a main course too.

Most businesses will gladly sacrifice a small cost (the actual cost of the dessert is much lower than what the client would pay for it) for the potential of additional business.

From your point of view, mailing a flyer to a client on their birthday shows you care for them and brings your business top of mind between visits. Resist the temptation to put any kind of physio messaging with the flyer. Instead, attach a note that says something like:
- "Just wanted to let you know we're thinking of you on your birthday. Enjoy a free dessert with our compliments."

In addition to the benefits for the client of receiving the gift from you, there is also a high likelihood that other people will hear about what you've done for the client.

Since it's likely that your client will invite others to go to the restaurant with them, it's inevitable they'll discuss with the client where the free dessert voucher came from. This gives you a nice bit of extra PR in the process.

If the idea of approaching other businesses seems too daunting, at Physio Marketing Solutions we've developed a script for you to use when you visit. Head to www.physiotherapymarketing.com. au and send us a note asking for a "free business referral script."

29. BECOMING BEST BUDDIES WITH YOUR LOCAL SPORTS TEAMS THE FAST AND EASY WAY

Unless you don't like doing physiotherapy on athletes, building relationships with local sports clubs can be an excellent source of new clients. As goes sports, goes sporting injuries.

Similar to approaching other businesses, it's important to quickly identify to clubs that you're neighbours (and not sales people) and that you're here to help.

Knowing who to talk to in the club can be part of the battle. Unfortunately, there's no one-size-fits-all answer, except to say that in smaller clubs, you're more likely to need to go further up the totem pole.

Without a compelling alternative, you may be able to advertise in the local school newsletter. For a moderate cost, this is probably worth pursuing but building a partnership, as listed below, is far preferable.

The following offers are valuable for the schools:
- Special offers/arrangements in relation to treatment for athletes
- Offering to come and educate their teams about avoiding injuries – a bandage-wrapping 'mummy-off' (where kids wrap each other in bandages to look like mummies) can be a good ice breaker
- Providing educational material for the club. To do this, you can do something like the following:
  - o Advise that an upcoming month is "physio education month" at your practice. Even if you don't have such

a program in place, you can create one just for the purposes of this exercise.

o   Explain that as part of the education program, you have some information that you'd like to get out to help the local clubs.

o   Discuss data about sports injuries in a compelling manner, e.g. "Latest data shows that spinal injuries and broken bones are on the increase in xyz sport, so it's really important we let clubs know what's going on."

Building partnerships with clubs is well worth the effort as a potential ongoing source of new clients.

30. HOW TO GET CLIENTS SINGING YOUR PRAISES (IN A WAY THAT WON'T UPSET THE AUTHORITIES)

Having a good level of Google reviews is critical for the ongoing success of your business:

- Research shows that most clients will check out online reviews before deciding whether to deal with a business.
- Having a good number (50+) of positive reviews protects your business from the occasional bad review:
    o If you have, for example, 20 x 4-5-star reviews in Google, a 1-star review is not going to devastate your online profile.
    o If you have no reviews and you get a 1-star review (as happened to a physio I know), this is basically online suicide with the capacity to kill your other marketing efforts.
- As a side note, most clients do not expect your reviews to be perfect (there's no pleasing everyone all the time). The occasional non-5-star review is helpful.

As noted in Step One, AHPRA guidelines don't hold physios accountable for reviews left on websites they can't control.

The best way to get Google reviews from your clients is simply to ask for them. As a rule of thumb, in the absence of an automated system, you'll probably need to ask 10 clients for one client to leave a review. This means it needs to be an ongoing part of your business processes.

The best context to ask for a review is at the end of a happy appointment. The discussion could go something like this:

(after the appointment …)

- Staff: "How was everything today?"
- Client: "Fine thanks. I'm feeling a lot better."
- Staff: "That's good to hear. We love it when our clients go home happy."

"I'm wondering if you could help us please. Would you be able to leave us a nice Google review? The instructions are here (*hands the attached page*)."

"It's pretty quick and we'd really appreciate it."
- Client: "Sure, no problem."

As part of the system, be careful how people complete their reviews. At one point, some businesses had an iPad available for clients to enter a review. Eventually, Google wised up to this practice and penalised businesses with multiple reviews from the same IP address (internet connection).

While offering free Wi-Fi can be a nice gesture for clients, this is another instance where you need to be careful. You don't want all your reviews being left by clients connected to your Wi-Fi. The same IP address issue can occur.

31. USING TECHNOLOGY THE RIGHT WAY TO ATTRACT THE RIGHT CLIENTS

It's fair to say that in recent times, technology has dramatically impacted how we can target our right potential clients. Of course, in days gone by, things were quite different.

The approach historically was pretty much a shot gun. For the uninitiated, a shot gun shoots out a pile of pellets which spread out the further they get away from the gun.

For example, the barrel of a shotgun might be one centimetre wide. However, by the time the pellets hit a target 10 metres away, the pellets have spread out to about 20 centimetres wide.

So, as the analogy infers, if your marketing is a shot gun, you're basically blasting out a whole bunch of marketing "pellets" hoping that they will hit the target.

The problem with this approach is that a high portion of your marketing "ammunition" (I'll dispense with the gun analogies soon – promise) simply doesn't hit the target.

It's time to replace the shot gun with a laser.

One of the main benefits of online marketing is the capacity to very carefully choose who sees your ads. While some people consider this to be somewhat Big Brother, from a consumer's point of view, this situation is an improvement.

If you're a 19-year-old student with an interest in bike riding, then you probably don't mind seeing ads for bikes. On the other hand, you probably have no interest in seeing ads for retirement villages.

Importantly, for physios, what this technology means is you can carefully target which clients see your ads, thereby improving your chances of them getting in touch.

There are a lot of fancy sounding terms and confusing acronyms in relation to the suite of online marketing technology. But, before you're bedazzled by what's on offer, just remember, if the technology doesn't make your appointment book fuller with new clients, it's not worth the bits and bytes it's made of.

In the following section, we'll unpack the elements of the key electronic marketing options available.

32. TAMING THE TEN-TONNE TITAN – GETTING GOOGLE REALLY WORKING FOR YOU

The Google phenomenon is hard to ignore. There are around *35 million Google searches in Australia every day* and Google (plus, to a lesser extent, Bing) provides an excellent opportunity to promote your business, especially if you're in the number one spot.

However, something that is commonly misunderstood about Google is that while it may appear as one system, if you want to use it to your advantage, you need to **master four separate systems**:
- "organic" (unpaid) search results
- Google Business Profile – a separate system, the content of which feeds into Google Maps
- Google Maps – appearing below the ads. If you're searching for a business, the map will show a maximum of three businesses in a given area that match the search.
- Google Ads – paid ads, typically appearing at the top and bottom of your search results.

We'll look through these elements one by one. Before we do so, let's have a deeper look at how a search engine works. In Aussie-speak, here's a "mugs' guide to Google."

How does a search engine work?

Before I answer this question, a little history. Do you remember life before search engines? I guess we bought encyclopedias, used CD-ROMs, or asked people in the know when we wanted to find something out.

When online search engines first appeared, there were a lot of them. I can remember personally checking about five search engines every time I did a search. Fast forward to today and it's a very different story.

These days, in Australia at least, Google is the overwhelming winner, attracting around 94% of all online searches.

In answering the question "How does a search engine work?" there are three key things to know.

1. RELEVANCE AND KEYWORDS

The one word that drives search engines is "relevance." Google basically won the search engine race because it more consistently produced relevant results to search queries than its competitors.

If you think about it, why (in years gone by) would anyone check *five* search engines? The answer is a combination of (i) not trusting the answers provided and (ii) not getting relevant results.

The way that Google drives relevance is through "keywords." Perhaps incorrectly named, keywords (or key phrases) are the *exact words that someone types into Google.*

As part of its relevance agenda, Google will produce different results for "local physio" to "physio in Sydney" to "physio near me" to "who's a good physio near me" and so on.

To ace Google, you need to dominate all/most of the keywords that people use when they're looking for a business like yours.

2. A MACHINE NOT A PERSON

The second factor to bear in mind when considering how search engines work is that it's not a person checking the now literally *one billion websites globally*, but a machine or "bot."

Often, people assume that someone will look up your site and decide how relevant it is for various keywords. (I don't think I'd like that job!)

The reality is no person is looking up your website to determine its ranking. Instead, Google's bot does it – a bot that is using possibly the most sophisticated formula on the planet.

The upshot of this is that in the past, it was possible to fool Google into giving your website a high ranking. In recent times, however, this has become much harder, if nigh on impossible. And, if you did succeed and got caught, your site could be blacklisted and not shown at all.

3. SECRET HERBS AND SPICES

With all this focus on relevance and keywords, you'd think it would be simple to get your website to appear first in Google, but not so. To help, let me tell you a story.

When I was a kid, KFC (Kentucky Fried Chicken as it was then) used to advertise that there were *11 secret herbs and spices* that gave KFC its unique taste. The exact recipe for fried chicken was a well-kept secret and this secret recipe was a source of significant public (and competitor) interest.

Fast forward to today and you can consider Google's algorithm (complex formula that search engines use) to be something like the secret herbs and spices.

For KFC, it was *11* secret herbs and spices. However, Google has indicated they take into account **over 200 factors** in determining what search results to produce.

What this means is no one (other than a few company employees) absolutely knows how the algorithm works. In fact, before a US Senate Committee, Google bosses admitted that around 1,000 people work full time on the algorithm.

However, with trial and error and systematic review, it is possible to find what's more likely to work.

To back this up, at Physio Marketing Solutions we guarantee the *results* you'll get for an agreed set of keywords in a given timeframe (typically 12 months). For example, if visitors to your website don't grow by say 40% or 80% over a 12 month period, *we'll work for you for FREE until we achieve that.*

Now that we've got the basics cleared up for Google, let's have a quick look at the four Google elements I mentioned.

Organic search results

Even though they don't appear first in most Google searches, organic (unpaid) results theoretically represent an independent, unpaid and unbiased view on a particular topic, as they are not paid ads. Of course, there are enormous benefits in being the number one listing for a given search result, e.g. "Melbourne Physio."

Of all the clicks received for organic search results in Google, websites that are in first place are likely to be clicked over 30% of the time. On the other hand, if your website is listed in tenth place, or worse – on page two, this percentage plummets dramatically to one percent or less.

A study by Backlinko.com found that sites ranked number one typically have *10 times the clicks* of the tenth ranked site. Rankings do matter.

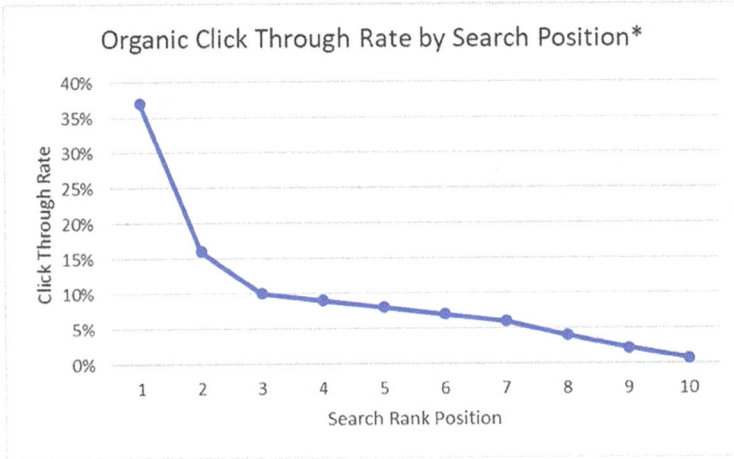

Organic Click Through Rate by Search Position*

Figure 1 – An example of common click through rates; actual rates can vary.

With such disparity of so-called "click-traffic" from Google, boosting your practice's ranking in Google is a high priority for most businesses, but not simple.

Unfortunately, despite the unpaid nature of organic searches in Google, winning the organic keyword race typically does involve handing over some cash:

- One of the 200 factors that influences search results is, in fact, Google (paid) Ads. Ads are a *factor* for search results but aren't the be all and end all.
- For most businesses, improving organic results means paying an outside firm to undertake search engine optimisation (SEO). Given the complexity, SEO is best left to the experts.

While it's almost impossible for businesses to work on these 200 factors simultaneously, there are some common themes that help enormously in getting a good ranking:

- The first aspect for higher Google rankings is *high quality content* relevant to the topic you're targeting – build your web pages with certain keywords in mind. The length of time visitors spend on the page tells Google about the quality of the content – longer visits are better.
- The second aspect for Google is *links from other, "high authority" sites*. Google isn't casting a human eye over your website, so they rely on other factors to tell if the site is worth ranking highly. For example, a link from The Age (newspaper) website has higher authority than a link from a new site with low traffic.

The implication of getting your SEO house in order is significant. For example, most practices we work with experience around double the website visits after getting SEO happening for around 12 months. More visitors equals more clients.

Google Business Profile

For a search on a topic related to business (e.g. local physio, lawn mower repairs etc), Google includes a partial Google Map in its search results. The information that is shown (once the person clicks on one of the businesses featured) is the information recorded on your Google Business Profile page (formerly called Google My Business).

If you don't have a Google Business Profile (GBP) page, you're not going to appear on the map. First you need to "claim" the page – Google will mail you a physical postcard with a special code on it. Then, there are a number of things you want to have as up to date as possible, such as your contact details, photos and reviews.

The features in GBP vary over time, including the capacity to create a "post" to advertise a promotion or event, add content, videos and so on. These features are shown when someone clicks on one of the businesses on the map and can be a good way of attracting extra attention.

Google Maps search results

As noted above, for a search on a topic related to business (e.g. local physio, lawn mower repairs etc), Google includes a partial Google Map in its search results.

Previously, around 10 businesses in a given category would appear on a map that showed the area near where the person doing the searching was physically located. i.e. If you were doing a search while you're in Richmond, Vic, the map that appears will be in the suburbs surrounding Richmond.

In 2016, the map changed from showing 10 business to showing three businesses – amid much wailing and gnashing of teeth from the business owners who got left off the new, more succinct, map.

The question I am often asked, therefore, is how to get your business on the map. Given that Google is all about relevance, the algorithm is looking for businesses that seem to be well represented locally.

To improve your chances of getting on the map (Google doesn't publish any how-to guides in this regard), a local SEO campaign can help.

Local SEO is a combination of regular SEO plus boosting NAP listings (name, address and phone number) for a local business visible on various websites.

Getting your practice on the Google Map in your local area can have a significant improvement in the new client enquiries you get. Some of the data I've seen from our clients suggests the map attract more clicks for most physios than the top ten organic search results.

Google Ads

The final part of the Google behemoth that I'll cover is Google Ads (formerly called Google AdWords) – Google's tool for online advertising.

The key fundamentals to getting your online advertising working well are:
- getting your ads in front of the *right people*
- delivering the right *messaging that resonates* with the particular audience
- *measuring and calculating the return* on your investment so you can boost the marketing that's performing well and kill off the non-performers.

The benefit of Google is that prospective clients are coming looking for you.

> *By virtue of them typing in, for example, "[suburb name] physio,"*
> *they've already told you they are in the market*
> *for physio services in your area.*

You can restrict geographically where your ads are shown. In a metropolitan area, you can limit this to **around 5-8km from your practice** as people tend not to travel too far to see a physio.

The second aspect for getting your ads in front of the right people is to make sure the ads are only shown for relevant search terms (the *keywords*).

For example, just because someone's search contains the word "physio" doesn't mean it's relevant. They could be searching for "which universities offer *physio* degrees?" – a search that is very unlikely to generate new clients.

I shouldn't be surprised but it still amazes me how many physios forget who they're actually talking to – *many physio websites almost appear to be written for other physios!*

ALL CLIENTS CARE ABOUT IS THE RESULT (and experience) they're going to get from dealing with you.

Historically, it has been difficult to accurately measure the return on your investment (ads are not free). Online marketing has changed this a lot.

What this means is you can confidently know how many people have seen your ads and which ads are working better than others.

This ongoing refining of which ads are used is known as *optimising* and typically generates better returns over time.

At Physio Marketing Solutions, we've had a LOT of experience with Google and we are a certified Google Partner (a fancy way of saying we know what we're talking about; we've done multiple testing to prove it).

For our clients, Google Ads has been an important part of their overall marketing strategy. With some investment, Ads generates our clients extra calls every week from people who are looking for them.

A more recent development with Google Ads is a bit unpalatable but nevertheless worth knowing about. While historically, the results from (unpaid) organic results and (paid) Google Ads were largely unconnected, there is growing evidence that running paid Google Ads impact organic results too.

We've seen clients' organic rankings drop sharply when they stopped Google Ads, and get a boost when they started the ads. To optimise your Google presence, you really need both systems working to your advantage.

33. SOCIAL MEDIA MARKETING – WHICH OPTIONS TO CHOOSE AND HOW TO MAXIMISE YOUR RETURN

Your capacity to engage clients via social media is an ever-changing minefield. The organic (unpaid) reach of social media for businesses is almost non-existent. This is because social media proprietors want you to pay for ads.

And you can certainly target the right people to see your ads – no problem.

However, there's one really big difference between social media and Google.

With Google, the client has come looking for you. But …

> *With social media,* clients have NOT come looking for you. *Rather, you have to INTERRUPT what they're doing and get their ATTENTION (i.e. by using an ad).*

This requires **heavy use of images/video and a simple message**. Promoting some services is going to work better than others.

There are two main ways you can target prospective clients via social media:
- use your organic social media as a kind of second website:
  o   This is about reassuring potential clients after they've done initial research elsewhere.
  o   Some consumers will perform a final check of a practice's social media pages to get a sense of "What are these guys like as people?" before making an appointment.

- advertising to a very targeted audience of potential clients.

ENGAGING PEOPLE VIA SOCIAL MEDIA

While there are some elements of social media that can appear "faddish" (and that's true with some), the overall numbers of social media users are consistently strong even if the players can chop and change.

Here are recent figures on Australian social media use:[3]
- Facebook – 18.5 million users
- YouTube – 17.5 million users
- Instagram – 10 million users
- LinkedIn – 6.5 million users
- Snapchat – 6.4 million users

Each of these social media types has a different profile of users:
- Facebook and YouTube are both fairly broad
- Instagram has a slightly younger demographic than Facebook (it's now owned by Facebook)
- for a social media tool of significant size, Snapchat has the youngest demographic
- LinkedIn tends to be more work-related than social.

The list above could have extended to dozens of social media types but, in reality, the best bet for physios is to just focus on one or two. Otherwise, the risk is you become jack of all trades, master of none.

One aspect that's really tricky about social media is that what works can change very quickly. Previously, regular posting on your Facebook page would have been a good way to engage with new and existing clients.

---

3   socialmedianews.com.au – Apr 2023

A change in Facebook's algorithm means your unpaid posts are way less visible to people who have liked your page. In my view, some posting is helpful so that people know you're alive and kicking but if you're think you're going to generate a lot of clients this way, sorry, no deal.

However, the strongest play, by far, with Facebook is paid ads. They're still relatively cheap and can produce good results.

ADVERTISING TO POTENTIAL CLIENTS

Advertising via social media is a marketer's dream, particularly where there can be options to TARGET CLIENTS including by:
- gender
- geographical area
- age
- income
- interests
- online behaviour (e.g. visited your website)

What this means is you can be **very, very, very specific about who will see your ads**. On the other hand, traditional ads don't tend to work well on Facebook, given you've got to interrupt people to get them to take action.

As long as you know what you're doing, you can closely match the targeting to the particular type of product you're looking to promote.

Clients of Physio Marketing Solutions have experienced 100 new client leads in a month using Facebook competitions. Quizzes can be quite popular too.

In this emerging space, the skill is in (i) creating something sufficiently engaging to get people to take part and (ii) getting that level of interest to turn into action.

Client engagement with physiotherapy is probably on the lower side – contrast that with pets or travel, where engagement is very high.

Consequently, a campaign that says, "We're physios and we fix people," is unlikely to gain much traction. A much stronger play is along the lines of the following:

- have an offer (e.g. first appointment free, two appointments for the price of one, get xyz bonus with first appointment etc)
- drive people to a landing page – a one page website that is specifically about the offer
- as necessary, ask some screening questions to avoid time wasters
- ask them to book an appointment.

34. VIDEO KILLED THE RADIO STAR (AND OTHER THINGS)

I remember vividly when I was in primary school going to a friend's birthday party where one of the gifts he got was a single. A "single," for those of you under 40, was a vinyl record with only one song on it. Actually, if you turned the record over there was another song on the other side, but pretty much all attention focused on the main song – the single.

The song my friend received was *Video Killed the Radio Star* by The Buggles (one-hit wonders) and we sat around the record player, listened to the song and basically marvelled at how cool it all was.

However, behind the coolness of this old song (subsequently covered by The Presidents of the United States of America band in 1998) are two messages – one about video, one about change.

VIDEO

In an online context, the consumption of video is higher now than ever before. YouTube globally receives 122 million[4] hits every day and Generation Z uses YouTube more than Google as a search engine.

Video consumption is no doubt influenced by the broad availability of the internet, including in a mobile context. Cisco reported that in 2016, 55% of internet traffic was video, but by 2020 it was 80%.

What this means is video needs to be a key part of your marketing efforts too, particularly if you're looking to bring more new clients into your business.

---

4   Thesocialshepherd.com, May 2023

Clients do business with people they know, like and trust. Video is an invaluable way of building up all three factors, but in a way where you can record a video once and get ongoing benefits from it.

Opportunities with video include:

- Introducing the practice both in terms of what you do and who you are – the vibe is really important here. If you can address clients' concerns via video (e.g. around fears of pain, stuffy receptionists, and/or poor service), you're much more likely to get them to call.
- Showing the elements and benefits of various physio procedures – animation can be very helpful for people wanting to understand how more complex procedures are done, and why they should have them done.
- Welcoming new clients to the practice. One option is to get a video done from the practice principal welcoming the new client and giving them a video tour of the practice. This can be emailed to the client and helps build anticipation of the visit and an understanding of what to expect, reducing stress in the process.

CHANGE

The second message from the *Video Killed the Radio Star* song is around change.

If you're unfamiliar with the song, it talks about the fact that once upon a time, people consumed music/entertainment, usually with a whole family sitting together, listening to the radio. The advent of video, however, effectively killed off the radio stars of that era.

Fast forward to today, and the rate of such technology killing off older technologies is faster than ever.

While there are some elements that don't change much (e.g. basic human needs), the way to communicate with clients will keep changing. The question to ask yourself at this point is whether your current marketing efforts are keeping up with the times. For example:

- How mobile-friendly is your website?
- Are prospective clients able to communicate with you in a way that suits their needs, not just yours?
- Are you taking advantage of the best methods to communicate with your ideal clients?

If the answer is "no", it might be time to have a rethink (or get some help). Even if you're up to date in this regard, the reality is the job is never done. There will always be change brought upon us, and to stay still is to go backwards.

CONCLUSION

While the range of options in the marketplace can be confusing, in this book I've attempted to simplify how to get more patients/clients and higher profits in your physio practice.

While the specific take-home messages are covered within each section, the overall themes are:

- You cannot ignore your marketing or leave it to chance – the marketplace will pass you by whether you like it or not.
- Establish an integrated marketing plan – forget placing all your hopes in bright, shiny objects. Instead, get Step One (*Check*) and Step Two (*Count*) happening, then implement a range of internal and external marketing measures covered in Steps Three to Five (*Create*).
- Choose your messaging very carefully:
  - o Find a way to position your practice as being genuinely unique. Otherwise, you'll be treated as a commodity and will join the price-focused "race to the bottom" (a game you never want to play).
  - o Focus on the result you deliver for your clients more than the technology you use to produce the results (your clients don't care about the latter).
- If you're struggling to get your marketing working effectively in-house, get professional help. The reality is, it's the best businesses that are winning the physio game today, not the best technical physios.
- If you'd like to learn more about getting help with your marketing, visit **www.physiotherapymarketing.com.au**.

www.ingramcontent.com/pod-product-compliance
Lightning Source LLC
Chambersburg PA
CBHW071429210326
41597CB00020B/3709